LAUGHING GAS

OTHER BOOKS BY RUTH WHITMAN

Poetry

The Testing of Hanna Senesh
Permanent Address: New Poems 1973–1980
Tamsen Donner: A Woman's Journey
The Passion of Lizzie Borden: New and Selected Poems
The Marriage Wig and Other Poems
Blood & Milk Poems

Translations

The Fiddle Rose: Poems 1970–1972 by Abraham Sutzkever
The Selected Poems of Jacob Glatstein
An Anthology of Modern Yiddish Poetry

Essays

Becoming a Poet: Source, Process, and Practice

The Marriage Wig and Other Poems won the Alice Fay di Castagnola Award of the Poetry Society of America and the Kovner Award of the Jewish Book Council of America; *Tamsen Donner: A Woman's Journey* was a finalist for the Elliston Book Award; *Permanent Address* was a finalist for the Virginia Commonwealth University Competition.

LAUGHING GAS

Poems
New and Selected
1963–1990

RUTH WHITMAN

 WAYNE STATE UNIVERSITY PRESS   Detroit

95 94 93 92 91   5 4 3 2 1

Library of Congress Cataloging-in-Publication Data

Whitman, Ruth, 1922–
    Laughing gas : poems new and selected 1963–1990 / Ruth Whitman.
        p.   cm.
    ISBN 0-8143-2315-4 (alk. paper) — ISBN 0-8143-2316-2 (pbk.: alk. paper)
    I. Title.
PS3573.H5L38   1991
811'.54—dc20   91-13840

Designer: Joanne Elkin Kinney

for my grandchildren
Sarah, Lucy, Jessica, Rebecca,
and those still to come

LAUGHING GAS

It was near the Coliseum, RKO,
in the Bronx,
on a broad street lined with trees
where the dentist, an old sweetheart
of my mother's, gave me gas
for a six-year-old molar.

I laughed.

       I swam inside
bubbles of laughter
in a leather-smelling office,
while my tooth floated away.

Then out on the street,
on the trolley,
all the way home and through the night,
I vomited.

I vomited my lost babyhood,
separations to come,
the plane over Reno, buses and trains
pulling out, each future diminution:
hair, teeth, breath.

My grandmother said:
laugh before breakfast,
cry before dinner.

CONTENTS

9

11

PREFACE

Many of my shorter poems reflect the common experience of a woman living during the second half of the twentieth century:—my feeling of repression and vulnerability in the nineteen-fifties; my rebellion in the sixties; my growing self-empowerment in the seventies; and my confrontation with loss and aging in the eighties and nineties.

After writing the personal lyrics in my first two books, I began to see how I could transform some of my perceptions by speaking in the voice of another. I first took on the persona of Lizzie Borden, the alleged murderer in nineteenth-century Fall River, Massachusetts. I wanted to explore the anatomy of her rage. I then looked for other women and men whose lives could expand my experience and teach me something about courage and the ability to survive.

I found—or rather, they found me—the nineteenth-century pioneer, Tamsen Donner; the twentieth-century Israeli parachutist, Hanna Senesh; and, in shorter form, the obsessive artists, composer Robert Schumann and the dancers Anna Pavlova and Isadora Duncan. More re-recently, I have entered into an imaginary conversation with King/Queen Hatshepsut, the only woman pharaoh in Egyptian history, whose life seems to me a metaphor for some of the universal issues of gender identity.

In writing about these lives, I began to use a more extensive narrative line. At the same time I have always remained loyal to the short lyric, with its beautiful analogies to music and song. A combination of the two—narrative and lyric, like recitative and aria—not only gives me broader scope in my longer works, but also a stronger possibility of transforming and illuminating the lives I am writing about.

I'm grateful for a Fulbright Writer-in-Residence to Hebrew University in Jerusalem, where some of the more recent poems were written; for a two-year fellowship from the Bunting Institute of Radcliffe College, which helped me to devote two years exclusively to poetry and translation; for a National Endowment for the Arts Literature grant, which enabled me to follow the path of Tamsen Donner across the American continent; for a Rhode Island State Council Grant-in-Aid in Literature, which allowed me to complete my book about Hanna Senesh. My thanks also to Mishkenot Sha'ananim in Jerusalem, to the Mac-Dowell Colony, to Yaddo, and to the many fellow poets who have given me advice and support, especially my daughter, Lee Miriam Whitman-Raymond.

ACKNOWLEDGMENTS

Some of the new poems have appeared in the following
magazines:

American Poetry Review: Falling, 1924

The American Voice: Coming Home during the Second
    World War, Cruelty, Fool's Thread

The Bridge: Word as Window

The Boston Review: The Drowned Mountain

Choomia: Your Call

Confrontation: Uncle Harry at the La Brea Tar Pits

Crosscurrents: Net, Lake, Sieve

Harvard Magazine: The Promise

Helicon Nine: The Awakening, The Mating, Writing in
    the Dark

Hollow Spring Review: In the Jerusalem Bakery

Images: Foreign Tongues

Indiana Review: Messengers

Kentucky Poetry Review: Sachuest Beach, 1941

Manhattan Poetry Review: The Shepherd, Sunion, The
    Young Scholar, 1952

Ms Magazine: Eightythree

Newport Review: Anna Pavlova

Ontario Review: Cracow, The Wedding

Ploughshares: Chamber Music in Early December, The
    Mountain

Poetry Now: The Ruins of Tiryns

Prairie Schooner: Clara Schumann, In Nazareth, Losing
    a City
Present Tense: A Gesture
Sandscript: An August Morning
Sojourner: Seven Stones
Tendril: Basic Training, 1942
Virginia Quarterly: Laughing Gas
West Branch Review: In a Mirror

From
Blood & Milk Poems
(1963)

STEALING FORSYTHIA

I came back with the sun smeared on my hands,
A yellow guilt
Pulled from my neighbor's bush,
Ten yellow branches
Moist with guilt and joy,
Caged in a green vase on the piano top.

Each time I pass my green and stolen prize
I feel again the greening of my years.

I would steal light from any bush,
Rob any blaze from heaven for my vase,
Just as I danced once on your wooden floor,
Naked and sudden,
Whirling you in a waltz,
Or did you whirl me,
Shaking the yellow spring
From rafters winter-stained with penitence?

That's the way I'd always have my guilt,
Sudden, high, a theft of fire, a dance,
A secret flowering of forsythia.

ELEVATOR

This sudden box has boxed me in my life.

Airless, I watch the leapfrog numbers play.
It's a sly trick. They want to make me think
I'm moving to perfection, but

They're wrong. I'm merely standing still.
The floors themselves are moving up and down
While I stand loyal to my gravity.

Down and up the steel girders slide.
All those bricks and not one out of place.
They do this out of ignorance or pride.

I'm standing still. You see it by my face.

THE FLOWERING SKULL

Monger of melting snow, the lovegod death
Cried up my avenue, fresh melting snow,
Who'll buy my melting snow?

Young hair will fall, ripe pear will crawl with beetle,
Doors rot and latches rust, tall lilies fall,
All tearless, windless fall.

My jagged heart, pinned at the root upon
The very bone, my season's jagged heart
Hoards death and distance. Heart

To hawker of the snow: I'll trade you death
And distance for the promise under snow,
The infant season stirring under snow,
One season's rose for all your melting snow,
I'll trade you, trade you snow for melting snow.

Round

I keep my clocks a little fast
so time won't take me by surprise.

Lest crows tread harshly round my eyes
I keep my clocks a little fast.

I push ahead the hands of past
before the future tints my hair.

I race the hours through the air
so time won't take me by surprise.

Before the spider bygone dries
I cobble cobwebs on my last.

I keep my clocks a little fast
so time won't take me by surprise.

My Murder in the Mesa

No brakes. We rushed
Through the dark till a fence mushroomed
Up like a corpse from its grave, sudden and white,

Hurled up at us from its sulphurous pit.
You bucked, buckled, would not hit,
Quickly summed the infinite, and dove into it,

Rolled with the stars, roof caving through ribs,
Knees knocking giant boulders,
Palms stinging with pitch and cactus;

Rolled through the purgatory of bent metal,
Courted every thorn, pebble, nettle,
And came out into the heaven of caked blood.

And I danced in my agony,
Surprised, alive, brave to be lost
So that you would have someone to save.

SONG FOR MOZART'S DEATH DAY

When the world closes, let it close.
The wind still blows
the jester knows
desire still winnows.

I saw the skeleton die
but then with guileless eye
had not yet taught the creature how to dance,
dance with his singing pain,
dance in the ice and rain,
dance on certainty, caper on mischance.

Cut off the dragging flesh
it blinds my feet.
The bed will cheat
and misery repeat, and misery repeat.

How We Never Touched Shore

And from the birdless sea we rode at last
to land with a three-chambered, harbored shore,
with dominoe streets and geometric fields,
small hairpin posts, and in the night a dog
who cleaved the darkness with a coneshaped bark.

Such sound and order mocked our rootless keel:
what man has made, free of the sea, and mild,
his neat domestic hearths, his foolish tiles,
his fruit, his fanes, his nesting hens that sang—
from this the unschooled night and foreign stars
teased us at anchor's length.
                                    The distant piles
shivered before the untamed sea who turned
once more, once more toward acres null with salt
our ship's beseeching bow and weary back.

THE WITCH OF THE WAVE

a prescription for a figurehead

That's how my carver made me:
Breasts thrust against the hammer of the sea.

Against is my element:
Driven against salt spray, wind, the jaw of the whale,

Against ice, spindrift, I plow my body's death.

Wrenched from mortal wood
I suffered the pain of birth.

With each chip
That fell on the sawdust floor my forest fell from me.

To this the birth and loss of any voyage is nothing.

*The head must be carved in such a way it will
not hold water.*

*The body, curved in eagerness for flight, must fit
snugly to the cutwater, fit the curve of the bow.*

So did he bend my tree.

Now I spring at the tide, haul crews of whalers,
Anvil against the wave.

When I plunge in the storm, I rise like a diver, sheering
All water from me.

My hair steams with foam, my paint gnawed
By the maw of salt.

Tethered to the world's weight, I raise the hull,
My face high to the gale.

Gulls know me. Dolphins
Dabble in my wake.

Splintered and beached,
Shipwreck is not my end. I bequeath my lucky bones

To some young sailor
Bound for his next horizon.

Touching a fragment of me in his pocket,
He touches pain, danger, phosphorescent joy, knowing

I bribe the ocean for his safe return.

SONG FOR A VIGIL

The bells all suddenly are nine
Be light my leaf the dark is bold

Love hung all night on a sagging vine
His grape a burr, his leaf a spine,
But now the clocks are ringing nine

Love shook all night in heavy cold,
His song a cry, his kisses old,
Be light my leaf the dark is bold

He comes with feet as bare as mine
And helps me stamp the bitter wine,
For all the clocks are ringing nine.

Be light my leaf the dark is bold.

THE OLD MAN'S MISTRESS

The two old heads
on each side of his young deathbed, mistress and wife,
met headon. He asked for the Bible.
Perhaps it was to prove he was right, after all.
But his curly hair proved it, and the women
who loved him, and his graygreen eyes, and now he was
  dying,
by choice. The thing he insisted on,
choice.

Cancer, pogroms, ignorance, gangrene,
he chose the thing he was to die of.
It could have been too much love.
He chose a broadhipped blondhaired mistress
with Scandinavia in her eyes, far from
the racket of his four sons in the tenement,
far from the immigrant wife who scrubbed the stairs,
far from the Russian soldiers who took his oldest
brother to Moscow to be a goy.

She heard
the lullaby in his voice. She had slapped
her old husband, twenty years before,
for his feudal lechery, and left.
That was her choice.
And then she chose him, Jacob.
He let nothing come of her womb.

She wept when she saw
me, his granddaughter, and her would-be
greatgrandchildren.

But she baked bread
and scrubbed his sweet body in a bathtub
set in the Connecticut grass,
and learned a few Yiddish words,
and outlived him.

          I am my grandmother
with her four sons, her outliving patience,
her patient hate.

          I am my grandfather,
loved beyond usual lot,
stealing his delight.

          I am my grandfather's mistress,
tending the alien land he left,
with no face for the face she loves,
                    dying
alone with her lovely bones, her only choice.

Regina to Kierkegaard

Be bronze, be bronze, for now I know that I
Must beat my sparrow wings against you, deep
Bronze in the sun, the bright light of your craft
Must bruise my eyes and spin a burning net
To trap god's birds and flesh them skeleton.

I would have bound your terror with my hair,
Counted your grief, consoled your history,
And brought you sons. But now my farewell beats
Like idle feathers on their imagery.

The gull's breast falters back, the bronze ship sails
Its polar sea, breath's enemy, death's blood,
My reeling wing now falling far from shore
Must plunge behind your deep discovering keel
And watch you sing toward islands of despair.

Aubade

When sleep kaleidoscopes and every tree
Rings out before a cannonball of sun

Sharp music shatters for the birds to sing,
Breaking their bits of glass upon the street,
Green glass, mean clatter, lovers' mourning bells.

Your kiss invented me, but I forget,
So constellate my sky with stars again:
Planets burn brief beside our tides of blood.

Mean birds, to give the tattling sun report
And clamp day's manacle on dawn our sport.

The Night Fisherman

A landbound shadow came at night
Riding a diamond light.

The curfew water stilled my fear.
His rainbow spear

Faster than fish, a prince of steel,
Undid my keel

And savage splinters culled from air
Spitted me fair,

Until I danced upon his strength,
Up-arched my length,

And burst like joy beneath his eyes
In jeweled surprise.

THE LOST STEPS

Snow fell when my young grandfather arrived,
Behind him Moscow, Eden, Athens, Rome,
Bareheaded, eighteen, and a wandering Jew.

Snow covered up his footsteps leading home.

Defiant of history, he laughed his way
Through passover streets, under each arm a loaf
Of leavened bread. A forgetting snow that day.

*   *   *

The first snow was the laying on of hands,
Blessing and naming, while Eve looked up to see
The white erasure hide her Adam's land.

How she had come, how gone, when Jahweh smiled
Blew drifting in her brain. She turned again
Back to her dishes and her hungry child.

And those old men rocking round their ark,
Beautiful in their beards, prayed all that fell,
Manna or snow, be Jahweh's favoring mark.

And Leda knew, when feathers fell like snow,
The thunderous wings of God in bright sunrise,
And threw her arms around his swansdown neck

And served him in his passionate disguise.
But in God's ravishing, Mary had wrung
Her hands beneath the bird who brought the sky

To cover her lament. Not knowing why,
Except she thought she saw her baby hung,
Shrunken, from the rafters of the world.

*   *   *

Was that my garden where I sang innocence?
Was that my cross that nailed the patient Jew?
Were those my thunderous wings? Was that my swan?

I cannot bend my knee.
All, all is gone.
I live on the charity of history.

Part ark, part swan, part cross over her hair,
My daughter stands before a holy fount.
Snow falls before my eyes. I cannot see.

I cannot bend my knee. I would not dare.

April Vixen

Where sweet fern suffered the fox of desire,
Where vines had tangled the sought for fought for hair,
There with small nose,
Black, invading,
A fox little fox with a long combed fire
Of fur rose
And shook her fire in the bright noon fading.

Sweet in her jungle the scents were green.
Orange and green fell cool and moist on her lair.
A dagger of sun
Struck through trees,
A sun whose flowered haft would lean
And blade would run
Between the garden's golden knees,

Bright daffodil knees whereto a fox,
A plumed and white-tipped vixen came to bear.
Joy pierced her belly
From ear to tail
And dropped among the fern and phlox
In a mossy gully
A bright pelt who must learn to wail.

Within the cool of the latticed shade
Her nose recounted her seven who whimpered there.
Through fern and rue
Her bright black eye
Counted the cubs the season made.
What will we do,
O what will we do in the day when the pod blows dry?

Poems for Rachel

1. THE SEA FLOWER

To the changeling coral and pearl
The moon is a huge purple plum.
But the shadow under the kelp,
When his time has ripened to come,
Prays through the wave's fierce furl
And the seaweed's solemn ballet
For the moon's sweet harvest help
And the bitter power to pray.

2. THE PHOENIX

A flaming phoenix came to rest
Beside my tiny nursling's nest,
Womb-warm,
Womb-blessed,

He snapped his wings of fire and cried
The world is full of claws outside,
And tall,
And wide,

The sky is turning golden red
And I have come with flames outspread
And Hallelujah in my head
To toss you from your easy bed,
To toss you from your bed.

3. THE TIGER

And when the hours danced upon her face,
Bright time the tiger kept his ravenous cave
And waited for her hunger, her lament.

Small spousal star, who could not count his days,
Your flesh then felt the minutes in his claw,
And memorized, before his wrath was spent,

How he must garnish aeons with your tears
And dangle you beneath his brazen paw
To satiate his cubs, his hungry years.

4. THE BAT

The bat's dark wing over her innocent face
Whirrs, falling,
While the hooded cradle
Waits to embrace her fallen, fallen in sleep.

Tender and perfect, the mouth of my innocent
Under sleep's dark wing
Trembles, falling
Through wells of air to the dark ocean of sleep.

Sleep, birth, and desire,
Down, the mind's body through space
Falls, falls,
And clutches the traitor air,
Remembering fear and the ancient fall from grace.

Sleep, desire, and death,
Both aged and innocent
In the year's falling,
The falling years, all in terror of time,
Fall and falter in sleep, and the wings of the bat
Beat forever over the brink of the sea.

MY DAUGHTER THE CYPRESS

Sleep, little daughter, I'll plant you a tree
Even as grandmother planted for me,
One tiny sapling more for the hill
Where two little cousins are flourishing still.

Sleep, sleep, dream of the sea,
Your cradle's a caïque, your tree, your tree
Will be a mast to take you from me
Grown for the boy who fells you free.

Sleep, sleep, the tree is yet small,
An infant tree, not three years tall,
It mocks its sisters, flutters its boughs,
Hush, hush, it rains, it snows,

Summer suns lengthen your hair,
You grow tall, you move with care,
And from the sea bright blue and white,
A sailor whistles in the night.

But sleep, sleep, not yet, not yet—
The hull is carved, the mast is set—
Sleep one more night in Arcady,
My little girl, my cypress tree.

BIRTH DAY

Tenant of the terrapin,
will you go your way, I mine?

If I do a lumbering waltz,
and bank you like an airplane—

if the sides of your tank
tip and bank,

hang on. Don't complain.
If I wake before you do,

And catch your elbow in my side,
if I rise while you lie,

you can deter me if you try:
but I will launch you into space

some sudden horizontal
Atlantic afternoon,

and you will swim from your fishless bowl,
find the stars in your faceless sky,

And be my moon.

MY SISTER BLOOD

Once I was sister to that lioness.
Proud, she was proud in her haunches,
Her breastbone was tawny,
Her jungle eye hooked mine.

Now I must think of her thighs,
How the down trembled,
Stretched on a rack devised
To farrow her cubs:

Beads of sweat lay on her island face,
Smooth with pain.
I held her iceberg hand,
Touched the sun in her thigh,

The cub was not mine.

Now she has littered clear
To the edge of the jungle,
Now she's a queen
Whose voice reverses the aspen

Leaves like rain.
All paths have suffered her step:
No cave is too deep,
No pain too dark.

But turning in sleep,
I meet her again,
Shaking,
Eye to eye,

And stroke the violence from her golden thigh.

HER LIFE WAS IN MY HANDS

From Sappho to the girl upon the moon
Sitting three centuries from now, I burn
With hot winds from the
Gutters of the earth.

We three were swimmers poised to dive
In catastrophic seas
Where down beneath the surface of those eyes,
Where worlds pull, where dead stars yearn,
My wrecked and whitened timber
Lies embraced in fern.

And she who from the cold sphere gazes down
Weeps to see me swim through outer space,
My very veins translated
To pregnant universe.

And she who gazes up through tidal trees,
Against the ocean's palm that weighs me down,
Cries me to rise, still dreaming to remember
The flooding terror of the moon's embrace,
The birth to come, the sting
Of comets on my face.

ANTIPHONAL

that first pang of air
daggered me fish to man.

                Child of my dark, you
                And I were almost one.

all the walls fell away.
nothing held me

                Now my body and I are
                Almost two, part

but the giant light,
and I fell, or flew

                Catapult for your despair,
                And, for your anger and alarm,

then drew my brandnew breath

                Part suckling heart.

and screamed.

TOURO SYNAGOGUE

As to an unknown lover I returned
To my father's land, a shifting land, now jeweled
And satined like a bride, a holy ark.

A stranger to his house, I heard my talk
More friendly to the twelve Ionic trees
Than to the tribes of Israel, more shy

To celebrate this birthday than to die.
White and perfect, starred with candlelight,
The sacred chamber held a secret stair.

The heart's escape leads out to everywhere,
Nowhere, but dreams still find a certain black
Connecticut hill.   My grandfather stands tall

And wraps me in his cemetery cloak,
Encircles me against the nightmare chill,
Till gowned in fear I follow with his ghost

Through village, town, down through the midnight past
To a second son reading by candlelight
Forbidden books that set his future free,

To an immigrant tender in his blasphemy,
Bold, repentant, joyful against death,
Rich in gesture, eloquent as earth.

Ignorant of all, I catch my breath
To hear the sharp crack of the shattered cup.
Driven to live, I grope to gather up

The windless torch of love, my tribe's rebirth.

From
The Marriage Wig
and Other Poems
(1968)

It was the custom for the Jewish bride in
eastern Europe to shave her head—as a
sign of modesty, or submission, or to
make her beauty less distracting to her
husband; she then wore a marriage wig
(sheytl) in place of her own hair.

A Spider on My Poem

Black one,
I was going to frighten you away,
but now I beg you,
stay!
You're what I need.
This poem needs real legs, faster than the eye.
And a belly with magic string in it
made from spit,
designed to catch and hold whatever flies by.
Also, the uninvited way
you came, boldly, fast as a spider,
till you paused all real in the middle of the page.
Everything I need.
Please stay.

Tall Grasses

Now too I hold my arms up
when grasses grow higher than waist-high
and the shadow still runs out of me
   crying, a child of six, lost in the grasses,
   and I taste the tears of green saliva
from a bent blade scratching my thigh

The green is too high. Like the hostile fingers
the day I saw my mother cry
in the mirror, saw her lost in her weather,
   lost in a field of hurricane,
   lost in a jungle of blades like knives
where the grasses grow too high

SPRING

When I was
thirteen I
believed that
the mailman
had sperm on
his hands and
if he touched
me I would
be pregnant
if he brushed
against me
in the hall
from my pores would sprout twigs branches leaves
buds blossoms unfurling I'd be an apple
tree in my white wedding dress swelling
the room until flowers exploded into the street
and rose up filling the sky blowsy with
fruit to come

LISTENING TO GROWNUPS QUARRELING

standing in the hall against the
wall with my little brother, blown
like leaves against the wall by their
voices, my head like a pingpong ball
between the paddles of their anger:
I knew what it meant
to tremble like a leaf.

Cold with their wrath, I heard
the claws of the rain
pounce. Floods
poured through the city,
skies clapped over me,
and I was shaken, shaken
like a mouse
between their jaws.

PERSEPHONE TRAVELS BACK TO HELL, AS ARRANGED

So long as this old subway keeps going,
I'm all right,
but it's the sudden stopping, the pause
in the middle of no air, nowhere
that gasps me.

Traveling back to a first rape,
cold and self-kidnapped,
I feel blunt and dulled.
It seemed truer, the first violence.

* * *

Snatched up in my father's Packard, his ancient troika,
crouched by his side,
we went plunging through the curving
Vermont hills
at what I thought was a fast clip, forty
miles an hour;
learning winter, forced to surrender
to one direction,
I learned the high glee of being driven,
ridden by a man.

The road ate itself up like a snake with its tail
in its mouth,
the world was one great perilous snake of a
roller coaster.

* * *

Now in my smart new winter coat,
orange, the color of sunsets,
and a hat made from a lamb
slaughtered half a world away;
packed lightly in one suitcase

so I won't need a porter,
I buy passage on his bankrupt line.

My gratitude to the black guts of the earth,
my thanks to this submachine taking me into the
    tunnel.
I brush kisses from my fingertips to all bats, roots,
    moles,
all blind and upsidedown things
squatting and squinting in the waiting dark.

Rachel Waking

She's in a well,
the walls covered with
slippery moss between
wet stones.
Under the water asleep,
holding her breath.
The clock strikes,
shooting her to the surface.

Her nose and the top of her head break through to air.
She scatters the scum lazing on the surface, the dragon-
fly resting, the flat leaf of autumn.

She climbs,
sliding up the slippery walls,
dreams clinging to her ankles.
She wants to fall back.

But up there standing in crisp grass, Jacob
waits by the well, leaning his elbow against
the day, tossing idly in his hands
her brand new morning.

APPLES AND BARNS

There was a time of apples and barns
Pastures and lawns, parsing
Latin parsing kisses in the sweet

Smell of hay.
                    They brought us back
From the heavyappled orchard, shamefaced,
In the back of the hired man's truck.

I watched the apples rolling down the sorter,
Small from big. Parsing apples,
You must look for yourself in barns.

Remember the pasture near the orchard,
The good smell of manure and boysweat,
When I blew over you petaled like a flag?

We said we'd be buried there.
I looked for myself in orchards, pastures,
Barns, I looked for myself among

Brown shoulders green eyes.
I remember your white boythigh.
And I came to an allnight barn

Freckled in moonlight, heavy with hay.
Leaning across fields and pastures,
You leaned on me. I began to be parsed.

Infinitive. The apple to be.

IN THE LOBBY

In the lobby while people shook hands
and flashbulbs of friendship popped like smiles,
while you said hello and hello to everyone
who didn't matter and I stood stylishly by
pretending I didn't know you
suddenly
I took my machine gun and,
dressed as I was in maroon velvet,
mowed down the popular lecturer with
his witty charm and good wife,
his friends, clingers, all parasites
and passersthrough, all those related to me
by birth, marriage, and death,
until finally I could see the ceiling.

The walls were absolutely bare and solitary.
Across the tiled floor only you were left.
You smiled, took my arm, and we
began to go home together

CUTTING RAPUNZEL'S HAIR

Rapunzel, locked in her tower, learned
to let down her hair and become
a ladder to her secret self.

> And the witch,
> climbing the secret every day,
> knew a prince would soon follow behind her.

Rapunzel, Rapunzel, let down your hair,
open your windows and doors,
let in the sun. And beware.
Loosing your hair is telling
your magic name.
Winter is watching you.

> The angry witch
> lopped off Rapunzel's braids
> and blinded the prince so he couldn't find her.

Some say it ended another way.
But now what girl would dare unbind her
magical, her sorry hair?

THE NUN CUTS HER HAIR

The nun
bald as
a uniform
offered her
hair to
her endless
Bridegroom.

And He
caressing as
air as
the sea
remembers winter
remembered
her hair.

A Daughter Cuts Her Hair

Once upon a time
a cat princess,
wanting to grow up,
cut off her golden hair,
and as it floated to the floor
babyhood
dropped from her,
yellow years curled gently with the dust.

CUTTING THE JEWISH BRIDE'S HAIR

It's to possess more than the skin
that those old world Jews
exacted the hair of their brides.
    Good husband, lover of the Torah,
    does the calligraphy of your bride's hair
    interrupt your page?

Before the clownish friction of flesh
creating out of nothing
a mockup of its begetters,
a miraculous puppet of God,
you must first divorce her from her vanity.

She will snip off her pride,
cut back her appetite to be devoured,
she will keep herself well braided,
her love's furniture will not endanger you,
    but this little amputation
    will shift the balance of the universe.

THE MARRIAGE WIG

If you're going to marry, make sure you first know whom you're
going to divorce.

—Yiddish proverb

1.

The Mishnah says I blind you with my hair,
that when I bind it in a net
my fingers waylay my friends;
that in a close house I shake loose
the Pleiades into your kitchen.

How can I let you see me, past and future,
blemishes and dust? Must I
shear away my hair and wear
the wig the wisemen say? Will you
receive me, rejoice me, take me for your wall?

To any man not blind, a wig is false.

2.

Once upon a time I wrote a boy
into my calendar of weddings. We lived
in a gargoyle house with many eyes.
Snow furred the street lamps. Inside
we had our wine, one pot, an innocent fire.

Now the gargoyle house is gone. On a tree
is the orphan number, forty-nine, meaning
49, a house, a marriage, a time
scythed clean, crunched to powder, flat
as a grave, as though we'd never been.

Let me apologize for that lost number.

3.

Let me apologize for all the faces
I've worn, none of them my own.

See me in my glass. A ghost looks back,
a witty ghost, who counterfeits my mask,
wearing a marriage wig made of my hair.

Inside, I'm threaded on a passion
taut as a tightrope. Strip away the hair,
the tooth, the wrinkle, the obscene
cartoon that decades scrawl—
underneath I'm naked as a nun.

I wear that nakedness for a disguise.

Ripeness

You wake up feeling
like an oven
where bread
has just been baked.

All night the yeast rose
and at dawn
you baked the bread,
a round full loaf.

REUNION

After the division the two parts of man, each desiring the other
half, came together, and threw their arms about one another
eager to grow into one . . .
        —Plato, *Symposium*, translated by B. Jowett

when your skin is strapped
to my bones, when I breathe
with your breath, wear your small
of the back, smile, eyelashes,
I'll be home again:

but I might cry for your marrow,
parching for your tongue,
and you might still turn away,
fearing the smart of my going,
so slowly grows our grafting—

until your sex takes mine,
finally, as it was
before the beginning, before
the pregods envied us
and split in two our one

DAVID'S BREATH

let's celebrate the
breath and airs
of love. David's
mouth, pastures of
honeysuckle, the nape
of his baby
neck, crops of
clover. Leda's hair
newly washed, a
thicket of balsam.
Under your arm
a decanter of
spices, the slope
of your torso,
newly cut wood.
And your sex
spilled over, like
barnfresh milk, like
warm brandy, like
David's breath

SUMMER THUNDERSTORMS

She walked bravely down the country road
every late afternoon

but she was frightened before it began. Protean
mountain shadows had moved

around her all day, a young bride
whose mother had now grown old.

Womb shapes gathered over the mountains, tongues of
electric snakes licked

the sky, just as she came back to the house,
lit the fragile lamp,

and began to get the meal. The house had stood
two hundred years, but brides

can't believe they'll live in history.
When the roof seemed to split

with the first crack of the daily storm, her throat
became cement. The table

was only half set, the potatoes just
boiling, but she sank
sank again into the sky's cauldron.

71

THE WAX DOLL

Simple the eye
that sees the moon
lurch down the sky
and crack the pool
if snakes should go
a midnight journey
and mad dogs howl
she'll only say
she gave a finger
nail away.

She's wax beneath
the sorcerer
who fingers and
transfigures her
and when she tells
her secret name
then every toad
will croak the tale:
how belly swells,
wits curl,
and shame curdles
a real girl.

SITTING FOR A PICTURE

The painter
narrows his
eye, measures
along his
finger, looks
at her up-
sidedown then
backwards in
a mirror.

Not touched the
girl on the
couch begins
to wear his
grammar. Per-
spective flat-
tens her curves
buttock brow
she becomes
more than her
self, catch for
a palette.

She gives off
faint power
like perfume
or buddha
she sits in
his eye like
an apple.

THE ACT OF BREAD

Some practice is required to knead quickly, but the motion
once acquired will never be forgotten.
  —"Water Bread," *The Boston Cooking-School Cook Book*
                              by Fannie Merritt Farmer, 1898

That happy multiplying
should have lasted all night.
But long before dawn
my batter crawled up the walls.
The trouble was, I let my secret
passion run into my thumbs:
into my own
flour yeast water I plunged my lust
up to the elbows—pounding the white
buttocks of my children, turning
their rosy heels; kneading the
side, loin, groin of him
to whom I long owed this caressing.

But before I could give form to desire,
invented flesh outran me.
It towered in my biggest bowl,
flowed over table shelves floor
till I scooped it up, frightened at my power,
and tried to hide it in a paper
bag. In an hour
it burst the side, climbed
out the window, through the door.

If I had baked that dough,
a crumb would serve as aphrodisiac:
one slice of bread
would people a continent.

                    But in panic
I carried it outside, bucket by bucket,
and gave it to the cold November morning.

SHE DOESN'T WANT TO BRING THE TIDES IN ANY MORE

Every time she tugs the sun across the sky
some old wound
comes apart at the seams.
But housekeeping by the clock means keeping
every star prompt. She puffs along,
blowing a strand of graying hair out of her eyes,
but she gets each planet to its place
on time. She bruises a hip
moving all this furniture around.

She steers clouds, fans winds, and slices
or mends the moon, according to the day.
Worst of all is bringing in the tides.
One hand brings them in on one side,
the other pushes them away;
                              while her knee
keeps the tipped earth spinning on its axis
precariously.

No wonder she went away and sat down on a sand dune,
wishing she were grass.
If she sits still long enough,
rain will come to her.

A Sound in Cambridge, Mass.

Every late evening in the silence before sleep
there's a crisp latch
opening in the darkness, the creak of a door
and two sharp steps
out to a porch, a balcony, and a voice
calling two notes.
They're the first two notes of an opera, an aria
to a lost cat.
She sings them over and over like a bird,
a bob-o-link,
only I never can hear the words that she sings,
perhaps Sam-bo,
Plu-to, Ju-no, a trochee, ending in o,
she sings it
always the same, never higher or lower,
the same breathless
expectation, the same lyrical patience.
And the cat
on a fence, in a garden, leaping at shadows, chasing
a velvet moth,
hears his own personal two-note violin
and comes home.

ALL MY BICYCLES ARE EMILY DICKINSON

Perfectly oiled, her tires tight with twenty pounds of air,
delighting in her moving parts, she mows
a narrow ribbon up the gravel. In low,
aware of every separate pebble, we make smaller
revolutions, fighting gravity all the way.

Out on the flat, we shift to second, raising our eyes
and seeing the bird's-eye map of leaves, striated bark
under the blue proscenium. Our spokes
make a girlish click click as we lope down
the wide highway, watching everything.

Now in high, we start to take off. Leaning my soles
on her pedals, I lift slightly off her seat,
letting the wind take us. I name her
Emily. And now she remembers how once
God pumped his floods of warm diamonds into her.

SISTER PHARAOH

Hatshepsut, old girl, old friend,
man-woman, bearded Pharaoh,
we women too pasted on beards
and said we were kings.
We brought lullaby rules of commerce to the state,
we raised temples and wrote hieroglyphs
and got the men
to erect an obelisk for us.

Hatshepsut,
you crouch in the silent hall of tombs,
trying to be a riddle.
But we can see through your beard.
Beneath your terrible crown of upper and lower Egypt,
beneath your archaic stone smile,
our milk has turned to powder,
our breasts are two inches of dust.

Dancing at Delphi

Ribboning down the unpaved highway
from Delphi to Arachova,
a skein of men and women
full of cheese, wine,
Saturday night love,

lifts you off the ground.
Through their bodies,
into their fingers,
the earth leaps upward
into you.

Noonday in the Plaka

Walking up from a bulletpocked house—
the smell of urine, dust
rises from the crackedlazy
sidewalk, fresh
bread from some
kitchen and crisp
entrails frying.

Up the sheet metal street,
each jagged house is
pinged by white light.
The organ grinder plays *o sole mio*
on his gingerbread organ, then
the death dance
from Zalonghou.

ONE OF THE KINGS

Child,
the globe turns
tipped on its axis
half night half day.
At this moment
a lovesick assassin
is taking a wife in
Ghana; hit by a stray bullet
a mother of twelve
lets out her last
bubble of breath
in China; in Egypt
a future inquisitor
is crying his first
sharp cry of birth.
Here in our classroom
under the slanted roof
we're playing a pageant.
A crowd of little faces
tied in handkerchiefs
dyed seven different colors
move up the aisle toward
six-year-old Mary
and her doll. We recognize
the shepherd by his
crook and toy lamb.
Annunciatory angels
in coathanger haloes
search the audience
for their mothers.

Now come the three kings
bearing gifts.
The blackskinned one
eight years tall
moves through us wearing
a crown on his closecropped head.

Over his shoulders the purple
mantle spreads, sprinkled with
golden fleurs de lis. He walks holding
the flask of imaginary
frankincense. He moves
handsomely toward
the little stuffed symbol
unaware
of the torn god crying
betrayal and massacre.

Public Images

THAT WOMAN HOLDING OUT HER HAND
is lying under
rafters, sand, stone,
bricks, sticks
of wood, a giant
girder, a mountain.
Only her head and one hand
are free.
Her face holds
continents
of pleading.

THE BOYISH POLITICIAN
naive and human, his
tie askew,
seems to be explaining.
His jacket is torn,
his collar all in motion.
They have poured cement
into one shoe
making his foot
immobile.

AN APOLOGY TO THE LIBERATED INMATES:
my clean underwear
makes it difficult for me
to understand you.
At what point did you
stop filing your nails,
stop planning what to have for dinner?
Peeled from my house, my skin,
would I be
raw like you
sick like you
an angry
harp of bones?

OUR NEXT DOOR SURVIVOR
lives above the waist
strapped on a bed
among lilacs, tulips,
suburban cherry blossoms.
Her legs belong to those
black woods where
Jewish children
march, trying not to
cry at the guards,
at the sourfaced trees.

THE LATE ASTRONAUT IN THE BOSTON GLOBE
grins foolishly at the unmanned
camera. Behind him
the earthglobe dangles.
His shoulderblade
blots out the map of Africa,
his earlobe overcomes
the China sea.
We've caught him,
tipsy in space,
walking nowhere.

Let's give him
burial toys—
two planets,
one for each hand,
let's paint
an Egyptian eye
to steer his ship
as he passes
our old sky.

Her Delirium

The old lady
(a child of seven)
cried in her sleep
Stop beating me!
Zu hilfe!
Zu hilfe!
In the dark cellar
her sons had murdered . . .
And the policeman was punishing . . .

The bright light
slid down the white bed
and the little girl
saw her wrinkled arm,
her withered knee.
Which is me, she cried,
which body is mine,
and why are they beating
an old lady of eighty-nine?

Almost Ninety

The last time I kissed her
I held a thin sparrow
her bones were that hollow

Where did she get the juice to turn
her eyes, to laugh at her greatgrandson
singing her jingle bells?

Now for my little dry wren
a cardboard box could serve as nest.
Too frail for feathers, she took my kisses,

waving come back, come back again.

BICYCLING DOWNHILL

To all things God is possible.
    Tipped at an angle for angels,
        Leaning on my breakneck ankles,
I try to pin the dirt path with my eyes.

Nervous pebbles, mounds of sand,
    Twigs fly slanting up my wheels;
        My rigid wrists, grown to handlebars,
Hold me counterpoised against the road.

I'm holding back while hurling down,
    Tensing past each hump of moss, each
        Rock, each bole of tree,
Each yellow leaf. A tiny toad

Becomes a frantic stone, avoiding me.
    Birds flute past my windy ears,
        The slow sky spells me out,
More tilting than my spilling down.

Plunging, I abandon brakes, no hands,
    Whipped by my gravity, beating
        The dust, devouring hesitation,
Letting the reins go, the final reins.

A Burned-Out Engine on the Southeast Expressway

My pretty seagreen manslaying automobile
raced lightly up the long hill, scarcely
　　grazing the macadam.

Her heart purred under her hood, the even hum
of all her joints played fugue and counterpoint—
　　until she missed a beat:

She drove delicately, trying to hold back
the first rasps of disaster. The pistons were out
　　of time, something was dragging

under the tailpipe. A wheel had gone soft.
The dry clashing of injured bearings,
　　Jammed in mid-course,

her slain parts clattered, then stopped.
I climbed out of the car, pale and empty,
feeling in my belly—like sudden old age—
　　the ruined dry engine.

FOUND OUT
A fractured villanelle

There's a strange man parked outside my house.
I don't want him to see me spying
so I watch him sideways
from the window,
screened and blurred.
                  All I can see
is a shoulder, a white, a grub-white sleeve.

He's sitting, parked outside my house.
He doesn't move.
                  I let my jewel
of a rapeable daughter out of the door
and watch him sideways from the window.

He doesn't move.
His car is red.
He's been parked all day outside my house.

Trapped inside my head I think:
he's singled out the very thing
I'm guilty of.

                  I watch him.
Parked outside my house.
Sideways.
He's waiting.

THE MARK

Grandpa, when you
lay dying, your throat
wrapped in bandages,
I came to see you
after school.

You wrote kindly
on a scrap of paper,
What's new? and I,
blindly, Today
I got an A.

You smiled at me
for that schoolgirl boast.
You already knew
what I couldn't see.

And I'm ashamed,
still ashamed.

DEAD CENTER

for John Holmes

        A thin fox
sidled by with his stingy shadow.
Bees hung in air,
each like a chandelier,
hot pine pinched my nostrils.

You sat up in bed
wrestling with the fox's silence,
it isn't time, it isn't time.
I looked at your face with the sharp regret
a mother feels for her child
sleeping after the day's war.

They broke flowers on your coffin,
knowing you weren't there. The sun came out
and all your faces flared for a moment:
you weren't there.
I'll beat my poem into a trap
for the stingy fox, to prove
that you were here.

In the Smoking Car

That hatless chewed woman sending me messages
with her eyes, what does she know about me?
That I've had my last child, that my
clocks are stopping? That love still comes to me
like birthdays or Christmas, and a brushed kiss
can be a whole concert?

She is grayer than I, more toothless,
but she grins like a sister.
Do my sins show?
                        What deception
does she see through me?
I shrink from her wrinkles, her sporty air,
her certain knowledge, older than cats,
that I am pretending, pretending, pretending.

OLD HOUSES

I wear this house like a barrel
to cover my struts
and I see:
>the plaster's getting veined.
>Tender clapboards won't stand
>too much more rain.
>Inside
>the wallpaper's crepy
>where the storm came in.

Looking out from inside
it's hard to tell:
will a coat of spanking paint
make the trim seem new again?

I've seen other women preen
to the image in their eyes,
picturing moviestar lips,
a dashing lilt to the head,
>while in the mirror
>looking back
>an old mask
>props up its wrinkles
>with a kissed out mouth.

But I feel like a virgin in the dark.
I hear my voice like a child's
enter the telephone
and come out no older.

>How come this new me
>is looking out of an old house?

I BECOME MY GRANDFATHER

Grandpa, I
want to tell you
simply:
that picture of you,
the handsome one with
curly gray hair,
amorous eyes,
arms folded in satisfaction—

I have looked
at you since I was
a little girl:
my grandfather.

Today I thought:
he's like some friend of mine,
a man I could love,
a sweetheart.
And reckoned
I'm now older
than your picture
by one year.

DEPARTURES

The buses stand in slips like ocean liners.
I scan the driver's face for signs of kindness.

    Rachel, now taller than I, once asked
    (before she had breasts, when she thought she
        was Snow White):
    How does a man look to a dragon?

    And answered:
    the man is very small,
    the dragon doesn't care about him at all.
    He'd crush him with his toenail.

Brave as an eggshell,
I've come to see her off.

A bulky girl stands by
with stonehenge ankles.
Sorrow seems to fill her like cement.

Rachel squeezes into the monster Greyhound,
clutching her suitcase.
I stand in the shadows.

Beside me a tiny Puerto Rican couple
are waiting with their children.
The boy and girl are chalk-faced, hollow-eyed.
They never cry.
The mother looks sixteen, too young to worry.
She holds the little boy slung on her hip,
while under him a spread of urine slowly
stains her skirt.

Last night, love, when our bodies meshed most
    deeply,
I touched your face and knew,
across a highway of nightmare,
your sudden absence.
Traveler, you slipped away
as we lay side by side.
Come back.

The driver slams his door and starts the motor.

Stonehenge stands alone like stone, crying.

Wrong bus for the Puerto Ricans.

    As the Greyhound backs away
    I blow it an anonymous kiss
    and think I see,
    through the moving dark,
    an answering hand.

ALL PRESENTIMENTS

All presentiments
of dying are
true. The angel
blows in the wind-
ow and spatters
your bedsheet with
east wind and rain
and you pull your
comforter, ocean,
up under your chin.

You Outlive All Your Diseases
Except One

1.

Give me anything of value, the nurse said,
watches, rings, teeth, whatever
is removable, also your eye, leg, hair
no I said and there are no
hairpins on me either, nothing,
nothing, I am stripped
down to my self,
plucked like a chicken, punctured for oblivion,
in anonymous white worn backwards,
wheeled like secondhand goods to a stall.

Strapped under arc lights I see
a dark doctor who says he writes poetry
in Arabic. I sympathize with a kind
anaesthetist who can't find my veins. I halloo
my own doctor who like santa claus
with a black goody for me sends me
raw, split,
sailing into cushions of mercy.

2.

Name me the parts
of cars, pistons, spark plugs, axles,
tires, doors, roof, radiator, categories
of fallibility that will be eaten
by collision, rust, attrition, age
and lie
abandoned by a used car dealer
in a hospital of wrecks.

Grass pushes through that speedy engine.
A lazy beetle
on the steering wheel
turns imperceptibly with the earth's
turning. They have lost their counterpoint of motion.
Gaping like lepers
the old cars freeze
in insufficiency: sky, weeds.

UNCLE ATLANTIC

He sat me on his stony knee,
put his great foggy arm
around my shoulders.

I said:
Uncle.
Hello.
I need.
        I'm glad to see your vast gray
fastnesses
are still here.
I can't see any seagulls
in this rain
but I know
fishes and seaweed
are sleeping in your beard.

Teach me
calm.
He taught me.

I Laugh in Russian, Kiss in Yiddish, Bleed in Greek

I laugh in Russian, kiss in Yiddish, bleed in Greek.
Laughter up through the knees, full in the breast,
rich with potatoes and grass, as though
the world would never wither; kisses full of birds
and babies, tongues of morning rivers
running to oceans of light; blood
straight from the womb, the marble veins,
mountains and Attic plains bled dry,
the sea robbed of its rosy islands,
blood as the future's monument, thighs
of laughter, kisses to mark my trade:
      twist water, thrust fire,
      wring the truth from the walls
      and people the instant earth.

Shoring Up

1.

On a clockless summer afternoon
in a cradle of seahaze
cupped in the palm of a dune
a man sleeps, defenseless as all sleeping creatures are.

Medallion.

I wear that graceful icon
pinned inside my forehead
to ward me against certain disaster.

2.

Last night's explosion blew
the starfish high.
I looked out and saw
sharks swimming in the sky;
the shaken sky
shook my bed.

I pulled in my knees,
saw a hill in Greece
where two small boys
fished in the air for birds.

They cast their lines in the thick gold air
and reeled back finches and starlings.
The cameo sea grinned
as though posing for eternity.

3.
Propelled by old guilts,
cast up on a rocky shore,
I lean propped on my images.

The man sleeps, his buttocks curved like a child
carved on an ivory gem, his fingers
opened out, his tender arc
suspended in my eye.

From
The Passion of
Lizzie Borden
(1973)

On the morning of August 4, 1892, during an intense heat wave, Lizzie Borden's father and stepmother were found brutally murdered in their house in Fall River, Massachusetts. Their daughter Lizzie, a thirty-three-year-old spinster, secretary of the Young People's Society for Christian Endeavor and active in the Fruit and Flower Mission, was arrested for the murder, tried, and acquitted.

It is innate in the female psyche to bring blood, conception, birth and death into close connection with one another. . . .
—Helene Deutsch, *The Psychology of Women*

Q. I ask you again to explain to me why you took those pears from the pear tree.
A. I did not take them from the pear tree.
Q. From the ground. Wherever you took them from. I thank you for correcting me; going into the barn, going upstairs into the hottest place in the barn, in the rear of the barn, the hottest place, and there standing and eating those pears that morning?
—Inquest testimony of Miss Lizzie Borden, Fall River, August 9–11, 1892

We were talking in the afternoon, me and Lizzie Borden, and I says, "I can tell you one thing you can't do," and she says, "Tell me what it is, Mrs. Reagan." I says, "Break an egg, Miss Borden," and she says, "Break an egg?" I says, "Yes." "Well," she says, "I can break an egg." I says, "Not the way I would tell you to break it. . . ." And she did get the egg, and she got it in her hand, and she couldn't break it, and she says, "There," she says, "that is the first thing that I undertook to do that I never could."
—Testimony of Mrs. Hannah Reagan, matron at the Fall River police station, on the ninth day of the trial, New Bedford, June 14, 1893

The Passion of Lizzie Borden

1.

Heat cracks the skin of Fall River.
Soot hangs flat
over the moist city.

Pears
sweat in the backyard.
Sitting alone in the kitchen

Lizzie feels
chunks of leftover mutton
heavy in her

belly. Her father
has left for the bank. The ring
he gave her long ago

pinches her finger.

2.

Openeyed last night she felt
her blood pounding
the back of her neck,

> tidal waves from the sea
> that poured up the Taunton river,
> tore open the breakwater,
> ripped apart her corsets
> and pumped breath, air,
> sealife into her,

sunstorms, volcanoes, astral debris,
until she was pregnant with a pregnancy
that puts an end to wishing.

3.

She woke, thicker around the shoulders, heavier
under the jaw. The birds
had left the burning pear tree.

This house has killed the girl she was.
Narrow, gray, grudging in windows,
bare of guests or laughing,

the parlor's only pleasure is to lay out
corpses or tell tales of each new
disease, step by fatal step.

What holds her here, eating pears?

4.

In the August heat
she irons handkerchiefs for her stepmother,
heating the iron on the kitchen fire
in the black stove.

The center of the earth is always boiling,
and she must have the trick of eye to see
how she can liquefy
stones, trees,
slash air so she can breathe,
take life to make life, break
the blind wall open with her fist.

5.

She'll hurl this pear against the door
until its ripe meat splatters,
like flesh torn in handfuls from the bone.

She'll trap rage in her like a cage
trapping a bear. Not only where
her sex is, but where her veins
become its bars.

She'll think, as it draws her juice
to her nipples: *that channel is why*
I was made.
My roots curl under me
where they suck life
(I'll find the sun
I'll husband a flowering bough)

6.

this sprung and spiralled wrath
won't uncoil till she's invented death

Her father is napping in the parlor,
her stepmother is sitting
at the vanity upstairs.

7.

Shake the murderous mountains and dance
a step or two before I turn to rain.

Then in the sky that gives me lightning,
in that same sky
my meteor will hurl;
will singe the tops of trees and bring
spring to the dry hedges of the moon
and set a clanging in the world
and break
by twos
the timbrels of the stars.

      Who's to judge me? When I sleep I sleep
      curled on the shoulder of God

8.

At last
I feel hallelujah in my hips
my son the day comes out of me the morning

She raises the ax.

TRANSLATING
for Jacob Glatstein

The old man was cold.
King David, they said,
we've heaped piles of clothes
on your bed, but your feet
are still icy, night after
night. Let us find you
a girl, a young
Shulamite, intelligent,
kind, who can spread
her warm bones
over you. . . .

       Abishag's
black hair lay
like a shawl on his throat,
her breasts and belly
and her rosy thighs
rode his flesh
shyly all night.

He did not enter her.

But as they lay,
slowly warming,
his voice found her ear,
and since he was sleepless,
he told her what
he was thinking:

how a slingshot had won him
a great lopsided battle
when he was a boy;
how he slew his ten thousands;
how his soul was knit
to his lover Jonathan;
how he answered Saul's

hatred with mercy;
how he danced unashamed
before the Ark
with songs and lyres
with harps and cymbals
and made his wife angry;
lusted after
married Bathsheba;
got himself children,
was betrayed
by a son, a son;
how songs still came
to him. . . .

And Abishag,
after all those hours
of listening, the world
in his voice,
rose in the morning
full of spermatic words.

Bread Loaf 1941

1. R. F.

We drank beer, cheered
Schwartzkopf, rolled
in the mown meadow
and wondered
which poet to marry.

We played
on our plateau, heedless
of Hitler. And the
granddaddy
of us all,

shaggy as a bear,
wagged his white head.
His despair
was so wittily said,
we didn't care.

2. On Theodore Roethke's Lap

There was only one motion,
down, racing down the mountain
in a beatup Chevrolet

crammed with a zoo of poets
and fat round Ted,
the lowflying slug.

We clutched each other
inside that black box
feeling our way by guess

and by gosh, whizzing down past
devilmaycare trees and a brook
at the bottom of the gulch

calling its cool persuasion,
early death for nine young
geniuses, thirsty for beer.

Ted's large knees under
me, the smallest and youngest,
felt soft and warm.

"Remember?" I asked,
years later, "after your
papa's waltz?"

"I always got a hardon," he answered,
now almost at the bottom of the mountain,
the waters loud in his ears.

3. REBUILDING THE HOUSE

On the flat lawn of silence
we will take each red brick,
    each yellow clapboard,
        and put back nail by nail
    like a film clip in reverse
a demolished Queen Anne house.

    The Olympic highjumper floats
    in the air like dandelion fluff
backward to his starting point.
And we will take each syllable,
    each movement of the mouth, tongue, jaw

        no, before that,
        the breath from the chest cavity,
    the smallest muscles to expel air, sound
waves, voice, word
and build the house that held the
first marriage room the poem.

IN THE VATICAN MUSEUM 1952

Through a glass box, behind an Attic vase,
love face, habitually misplaced,
how you turned up like a clown
in the museum in Rome,
looking through to us
at the same vase
in the same case in the same room,
far from Cambridge, Salt
Lake City, all your warring
and contrary places.

Awkward body born from a candy machine,
you appeared and disappeared, sad
smile on a mummer's face.

Young and naked in March
we all plunged together
into the cold Rockport quarries—
and you disappeared.
                        I found you

gaping over a halfeaten banana
at the Spreading Chestnut Tree on Brattle Street.
We captured you in our furnished room
over a bottle of chianti.

You disappeared.
                Love,
in and out of windows, we
took a bus to Salem
and lost you again
among the seven gables.

                        Antic face
in the Vatican, how
did you come to be jumbled among
these antiquities?

PLAYING DEAD

Locked in a motel
of mummy light,
fake air, we breathe
plastic.

      Thin dreams
flick across the walls.
Voices quarreling from the next tomb
keep us
not quite asleep.

A splinter of morning
enters through a crack.
We pry at the slit
until an untamed
tiger of sun springs in,
pushing the door open.

We have the answer
before the question.

For David Sacks,
Odessa 1881—Boston 1965

Once in his jaunty middle age
his wife had caught him again behind the door
kissing the girl from downstairs. . . .

       Driving to the hospital we lied,
       They're going to make you well, you'll
       dance at our wedding.
                    His arm
       was still smooth as a boy's. You could hide
       your fingers in his thick
       eighty-four-year-old hair. Natty
       even in his hospital johnny,
       he basked in a flurry of nurses.
       But he no longer wanted to eat.

. . . Fighting years of cooking smoke,
counting children, pennies, sugarbabies
from the candy store she kept for him,
she locked him
               debonair as Odessa
in his room.

UTTERANCE

Miss Muffet,
perceiving the spider
beside her,

screamed.
She moved the tiny muscles
in her adam's apple, dropped

her lower jaw, and forced the air
in waves
out of her mouth

to my eardrums,
a minute thrumming.
She knew, as her animal ancestors

before her, that sound
carries well, will turn a corner,
can be heard in the dark.

I think I hear
through a musky orchard
the silent abdominal

language of bees
playing violins
to the bass sonatas of whales

circling the sea.
I'm threading these songs
on syllables of wonder, remembering

bekos, the Phrygian word for bread.

A NAP AT SUNION

Peeling away the layers of clouds,
dollying in with my dream camera,
I see

a girl
curled up naked
sleeping on a rock.

She has climbed down the spiney hill
to explore an ancient cave
chill with the smell of shepherd's urine and Poseidon.

She swims in the sea near a ledge,
never thinking of the octopus watching her.
She floats

toward adolescent islands
nippling the horizon.
And then she sleeps

while the horns
of the god's temple
rise over her.

DIGGING

centuries from now in the soil
of his city, the antiquarian will change
his story, partly guessing how rain
wore down the mountain
and how earth heaved up its double.

Layer on layer, the land doubles
back on itself. But all his digging
will not reveal the mountain
worn away or the soil
multiplied, or how rain
marries out his features. Change

comes atom by atom, an exchange
of smooth for rough, double
for unique. Each drop of rain
pocks the world's surface, digging
minuscule trenches in the soil
of mountains.

And the mountain
changes,
moving through air, water, soil,
like a juggler with a double
set of oranges. Digging
reveals he is not wholly lost, becoming rain.

The rain
pours down the mountain,
wearing away the scholar digging
through each change
of lifetime, through each double
city under soil,

wearing away the soil
itself. Pebbles rain
down, doubling
the ground he walks on. Mountains
of change
open beneath his digging.

Digging in the soil
of his city, he exchanges himself for his double:
atom, mountain, rain.

ZION

Grayfaced,
groping through the day,
I come to touch you breast to breast
and spring up, replenished, rosy
with your quickening.

Touchstone,
your body is my Israel,
your shoulder my wailing
wall, your face the bible
of my wandering.

THE THIRD WEDDING

On the way to her second wedding
dressed like a Christmas package
tinseled and laced with ribbon,
she caught a look at herself.

Her heart crashed with terror
under her champagne dress.
She shook from her shoes to her careful
veil.

Where was the minyan
of ten good men? The cup
under the bridegroom's heel?
The canopy of flowers?

When guests turned to the altar,
she shed her mistaken skin
and rose clear of the building.
No one noticed her missing.

She gathered ten years for a minyan,
plucked a canopy of planets,
brought her body like a cup

to the bridegroom long denied
who drew her to his side,
his rib, his final bride.

Four Poems of Comfort and Discomfort

1. AFTER THE ABORTION

Your knees, Uncle Doctor had said,
Watch those knees.

         Traffic,
tuned to Schönberg,
floated through
the August window.

I tasted flat peroxide
and death.

On a certain betrayed afternoon
I realized
the bubbling was my own blood.
Half a lifetime later,

twenty miles away,
I leaned my head on my hand
and aged.

         	

2. On the Way to Mount Auburn Hospital

Inside pain's white
balloon I tasted
every pebble and pothole
the narrow red truck
jerked over

The fireman beside me
with the vague family face
was saying something blurry,
but his hand holding mine
was dry and clear

3. DERAILED

that time the train
    heeled and yawed
I braced my angry back

against foot-
    loose evil, my long expected
adversary

His dark flank
    passed over
me

Stumbling to the broken
    door
I discovered

    I had lost my shoe

4. BELLYACHE

The night she had a bellyache
  she fitted herself into
    all his corners

    and spaces, wearing
   him like a bandage
against her little pains.

    Curling behind him
   holding his sleeping penis
in her hand

    she tried to become
    part of his
    architecture.

RISING TO THE OCCASION

Up! As Archilochus said,
soul, you must, despite all
annoyances, and this
vile island you live on, shaped
like the backbone of an ass:
despite this, up, wash, dress
and out.

Soul lies wallowing with a cold in her nose.
Her head aches. Fever. Loving enemies
come running with pills, chicken, exotic
remedies. All night there's a chill in the room.
Fever. War.

Up! Beneath the island,
vomited up from ancient
volcanoes, there hides a grievous
fault. But splayfooted soul
will rise. Her juice will spurt
again, again through a
dry stalk.

WHEN THE CHILD AT YOUR BREAST IS A METAPHOR

1.
At the pool
the young mother in the yellow hat
follows along the edge,
on land,
watching her tadpole child in the water.
Every muscle in the mother's dry body
swims, as her child paddles across the surface,
not drowning. She can't keep her hands
from stretching out. She moves
her feet along the edge,
dancing a pas de deux of terror
and separateness.

2.
The child's voice on the telephone
wavers and breaks
as the rainstorm breaks on the line.
Thunder slams the house.
His words,
jigsawed by lightning,
fall
apart
while rain
beats in the open windows
blurring the words
in her ear.

A Cry

A man is howling like a dog.
Is a dog crying like a man?

In your backyard universe
where clusters of birds sang like roses and
crows rowing through the thick air
have dropped their triangular cries,
someone is in pain.

A dog thinks he is a man.
Or a man is skinned to his animal.

K. 516

From your graveyard
on the moon, three
hundred thousand
miles away, you
look back
on your leafy toy
(diminutive, savage
as a child, round
with baby fat
and dimples)
and you think of a pulse
in the throat of Constanze
in 1782,
a mote in the mote
in the eye of death,
and out of your cinders,
across your rubble of birthdays,
you jig her a rondo
allegro, the broken
wing of a fly.

PAINTER

What's riches to him
that has made a great peacock
with the pride of his eye?
                    —Yeats

He sees into yellow balloons
        of sun.
            Dives
into turquoise. Swims
        under layers of blue.

Turns and walks
        around the trunk of a tree
flat on the wall. Drops a cat

between   the sleeve
        and the rib
of the portrait.

        Sees space.

Six oceandeep miles of it
        in a narrow room.

Sees.

        And holds Cezanne's apple,
like love,
            the round of it.

Laying a Fire

The fire starts when two logs meet.

They barely touch.

Close enough to draw juice from the embers,
enough apart so every tongue moves
freely.

       In a little while time changes the relation.
       One loses in the fire more than the other.

I'll step back.

       You
move an inch forward.

MEDITATION

Traveling back forty-five light years
through the middle of
your forehead:

tumbling over the edge of the medieval
ocean until you are
merely a

point of light in a black universe,
an absolute elsewhere,
an ovum,

a picture of an ovum on a black page
magnified a billion
times;

feathering off from cushions of sun,
you wake up laughing,
your laugh

tickles the edge of the galaxy,
waiting to be born,
to be

Lament for a Yiddish Poet

Jacob Glatstein, 1896–1971

1.

I want to fasten you inside my head.
Where else can you go now?

I'm sending you my strength,
I said on the telephone.

The telephone wires were laughing at us.

Words are all you left me:
they stroke my cheek, thrust under my hand

like kittens. I heard you shouting, you were angry.
But now I know you were frightened

and didn't want to die
here, at the edge of the desert,

where you struck voices out of rock.

2.

They put you in a pine box
under a star of David
and a few red roses.

The room was breathless
as a grave,
busy with worms.

You stood at the door watching
the coffinbirds peck at the poet.
And quickly left.

3.

In the air, on the wide sky,
you write from right to left,
dark and sunny,
sending me messages.

                   Adam and Eve
are lazing in a pool of blue,
waiting to begin.

Where are you?

                   With a Word,
with a flock of words dense as starlings
you wheel across the sun,
naming the first creatures
in a cantata of light earth sea.

4.

You kissed the face of despair.

I may live to be a hundred, you said,
but I will be dead for centuries.

The faces of all the children, the dead,
the burned, the living, the murdered,
the unborn, are lifted up,
are waiting for your kiss.
For the mother-tongue of rain.

CASTOFF SKIN

She lay in her girlish sleep at ninety-six,
small as a twig.
Pretty good figure

for an old lady, she said to me once.
Then she crawled away, leaving
a tiny stretched transparence

behind her. When I kissed her paper cheek
I thought of the snake,
of his quick motion.

PASSOVER 1970

1.

Athens and Jerusalem   cities of my being   the faces
on your streets are my face   the houses   the rooms
    inside
the houses   the beds inside the rooms are places
    where I
was born   made love   took in your seed

2.

    A child of many wars,
    how is it my tongue
    speaks only the vocabulary of peace?

3.

Now it is time to move out of the narrow space.
The I is the starting place, never the arrival.
The journey outward begins now

4.

    Inside Agamemnon's beehive tomb,
    the stones,
    square and heavy,
    fit cleverly together.

    The king was laid inside,
    a bled shell
    once warm to the hands
    of his wife.

    He was practical,
    he traded
    his child's life
    for fair winds, for war.

    Thieves have emptied his tomb.
    He did great harm.

And was harmed.
Words   Stones   A cool air

5.

When I was pregnant in the Athens prison, the colonels
beat the soles of my feet with sticks. I asked them
to be careful of the baby. They laughed and said
Another one like you? Soft and arrogant? And beat me
      more.
Afterwards I lay, unable to walk, weeping in my cell. In
      the dark
I felt a sudden gush between my thighs, and knew
            that I had lost my child

6.

      Tigers roam the streets. A crow
      Snuffs out the sun.
                  Babies
      tilt with hairpins at the president,
      who scoops them up and stuffs them
      in his smile

7.

Pharaoh's horses were closing in behind us.
We shouted and dodged in the dark, stumbling down to
      the beach,
shoving aside even our fathers and children,
trampled, half-drowning, cursing our foolish escape
      from Egypt
when Moses said:
            Stand still, my people. I must think what to do.
            Stand still. I will not let you perish.
            O Lord, you created the earth
            and the water that covers the earth—
            how can I, a mere man,
            separate the sea,
            reverse your plan,
            and give my people a safe path

to the other side?
Help me.

8.

Leaving for war, the husband ties his shoes
tightly, confirming the miles between
her bed, his chair.

                    Masada falls.

Lilacs fill the air.
Surviving lovers, barefoot,
multiply.

From

Tamsen Donner:
A Woman's Journey
(1977)

Tamsen Donner, a New England woman originally from Newburyport, Massachusetts, was a member of the party of affluent pioneers who set off in 1846 from Springfield, Ohio to walk across the American continent in the course of one summer, hoping to arrive in California in early fall, where free land was being offered. But like many American experiences, what began in naivete and optimism ended in tragedy. The land was much harsher than they expected; they took a wrong cutoff across the Great Salt Desert; and ran into early blizzards at the foot of the Sierras. Half the party was lost through sickness, starvation, and cannibalism, but Tamsen's three children survived.

Where is the West?
Who shall fix its limits?
He who attempts it will soon learn
that it is not a fixed but a floating line.
      —ELEUTHEROS COOKE, 1858

how could I foresee my end
in that soft Illinois spring?
I began my journey certain
that what was unknown
would be made smooth and easy

I forgot the anger of the land

now in the white silence I remember
wind blowing back the hair of the ocean
sunlight slicing through clouds
spring birds circling south

under the cities of snow
under the whirlpool of leaves
my beginning stirs again:
out of the white spring of my unbelief
a far blue country parts the sky

April 15, 1846, leaving Springfield, Illinois.

The wagons move first,
one directly behind the other,
but then straggling—
friends want to ride beside friends,
and we pass back and forth.
It is like a large summer party
  except for rumors that the Mormons
  who are also moving west this spring
  will massacre as many of us as they can;
  that the Indians will steal from anyone who
  separates from the train; that there may be
  war in California.
But we are surrounded by our friends
and at night outside the hollow square of wagons
we drown out the howling of the wolves
by singing hymns and old ballads around the campfires.

Just sometimes, when we are fairly on our way
one behind the other
undulating over the prairies
we have much the appearance
of a large funeral procession.

April 20, 1846, on the Missouri prairie.

The land flattens out most suddenly, long stretches of
flat fertile land, stands of young corn. The horizon is
everywhere. We picknicked by a huge flat field with a
sky broader and lower than ever in the East I could
imagine. Broad, low and blue, with herds of clouds.
The stretches themselves are punctuated here and
there with little isolated exclamation points—a house,
a barn, a shield of trees planted by an emigrant. Trees
show either that water is present or someone brought
a sapling to shade his house. Otherwise there are none.
Only immensity and loneliness. We change in relation
to the land. We become smaller.

153

May 26, 1846, on the Kansas prairie.

Where are the seagulls?
                    crossing
the prairie, I keep mistaking hawks
for gulls: a thick wind
blows inside my head full of salt
and seafog

          now in my dreams I find
wild rosehips on the beach
at Newburyport: I'm a child
chasing waves across the sand
sails sting white against the blue

in these feathery seas of grass
traveling towards the steep
heart of America, why do I
keep watching for seagulls?

June 2, 1846, along the Big Blue.

I find it awkward at first to bake out of doors but now
that I am becoming accustomed to it I do it quite
easily.
Our table is the ground,
our tablecloth an old India rubber spread,
our dishes of tin:

tin basins for tea cups,
iron spoons and plates
and several pans for milk

I find the wagon's jolting
can churn a pail of cream to butter
in a day's journey

June 17, 1846, on the North Platte.

The morning is fierce with fresh smells:
prairie grass   clover   and the familiar
lupin paler than the sky bluer
than the periwinkle starring the ground
around the stream under willows and alders

I pick the wild blossom and mark the joining
of leaf to stem the design of
petal to petal
                    and I remember
the kiss of fingers
the joining   the holiday of eyes
in an Illinois meadow

            I had brought my class
            to study the wildflowers
            not knowing the tall farmer watching us
            owned the field and would be my future
            refuge

            a widow of thirty-five I had thought
            my body would not stir again
            my lifelong fires were banked
            but in his rich earth
            winter buds unclenched their tightness
            under his sun his unaccustomed rain
            I shed my widowhood
            and let a new self burgeon

            husbanded again have I finally learned
            to let be let go? the need
            to find oneself within a man
            is not so great the second time

but we are like two voices of a strain
that come together and go apart
each echoing but singing independently
knowing the coming together in the end
will thread into a single theme

June 18, 1846, along the Platte.

We watch the land dry out. Trees grow smaller and
disappear. Patches of light sand, and then, on the
plains, long low hills. We keep crossing and recrossing
the Platte,—ugly, shallow, and as the mountain men
say, a mile wide and a foot deep.

We pass a dead ox and two graves of children.

We sometimes see
the shattered wrecks
of ancient clawfooted
tables, well waxed and rubbed
or massive bureaus of carved oak
sitting along the track:
once loved relics
flung out
to scorch and crack
on the hot prairie

July 4, 1846, at Fort Laramie.

Dressed in our best clothes, which we have saved for
this occasion, we come together in a grove and open
the bottle of wine our old friends in Springfield gave
us. They promised they would toast us today, facing
towards the west, as we drink to them, lifting our
glasses to the east.

> So do we make a link
> between what we were
> and what we have become:
>
> we are inventing
> the body of a land
> binding together
>
> two halves of a whole
> as we touch each other
> across a thousand miles
>
> and I who started
> a thousand miles before
> feel in my flesh
>
> the stretch of the land
> as we give it birth
> the long spill of it
> unrolling before us

July 18, 1846, crossing the Great Divide.

An end or a beginning:
is this the place where being separates
from itself the precise moment
the space between pulse and pulse

at one instant we are moving towards:
transporting the furniture of our lives
bringing the particularities of one existence
to an imagined point where we are taken in
formalized justified like an embrace
without an end

but no love is so final   merely
having traced ourselves back to our
Atlantic beginnings
we change from source to source
leap to a new love plunging westward
where once we looked backward all the way

now hesitant among the mountains
we pass across the invisible boundary
that divides self from self
and move forward heartlong towards the other sea
a twin
a mirror of ourselves

July 25, 1846, along the Big Sandy.

Thus we scatter as we go along
the arid stretches are so dry
the hills are so steep
that we must constantly tar
and mend the wheels

it would have been better
not to bring
any baggage whatever
only what is necessary
to use on the way

if I were to make this journey again
I would make quite different preparations
        to pack and unpack so many times
        and cross so many streams

the custom of the mountain men
is to possess nothing
and then you will lose nothing

September 6, 1846, in the desert.

Go light go light I must walk lightly

as I moved from one life to another
more and more followed me:
gowns books furniture
paints notebooks

now the seven of us—even the little girls—
must have substance
to carry into the new country

we are transporting a houseful:
barrels of flour stuffed with porcelain
pots tin plates silver service quilts
salt meat rice sugar dried fruit
coffee tea
              the wagon sags
and the oxen falter
                        one wagon founders

what shall I let go? books:
                        the least
needed for survival: in the cold
desert night
              George lifts my heavy
crate of Shakespeare, Emerson, Gray's
Botany, spellers and readers for my school
and hides it in a hill of salt
while the children sleep parched
and the cows and oxen stand mourning:
I put aside my desk with the inlaid pearl
our great fourposter with the pineapple posts
my love my study

what else can I part with?
I will keep one sketchbook one journal
to see me to the end of the journey

go light
go light
I must walk lightly

November 3, 1846, by Alder creek.

Stopped.
    We can go no further.
Here steep in the mountains
the flakes thicken down
heavier and heavier
the white veils swirl between us
and the pass

George with his injured hand
starts to fell the trees
to build a shelter
but the snow falls and falls
fat flakes
sent to wind us in a
thick sheet
we have no time to pitch a tent
we make a shed of brush
roughed over with pine boughs
rubber coats blankets and skins
the two little ones sit on a log
snug in a buffalo robe
cheerfully watching us work
thinking it fun to catch the snow
on their tongues

inside this strange
dwelling place
I must build a fire
and make another nest

November 12, 1846, by Alder creek.

The wound on George's hand does not heal. He feels
ill and cannot stand up, although he protests it is
nothing and will pass. The poison seems to be traveling
up his arm to his shoulder. I bathe it in melted snow,
salve it, bind it up, assuring him with all my love that
it will improve. But it worsens. I think it begins to
smell of decay, although it is hard to distinguish smells,
we have lived so long in this close wet space.

The children were glad at first to stop in one place
and play in the snow, but now they prefer to lie quietly
in bed, keeping each other warm.

So it falls to me to fetch twigs for the fire, prepare our
little food, and make the time pass until help comes. I
have told all the stories I can remember and sung all
the songs.

165

December 26, 1846, by Alder creek.

I have come up out of our black hole beneath the snow
(where the children sleep all day in damp clothing
and George lies without stirring)
to breathe the sharp white air

these mountains
comfort me
a blazing army
straddling the sky
with their long pyramidal pines
dark green black green
trees trees a profusion of trees at last
against the lake

these shapes these colors cleanse my eyes
and I turn back to our evil-smelling cave
a little stronger to confront
the next meal and the next day and the next

April 10, 1847, by Alder creek.

How can I store against coming loss?
what faculties of the heart
can I bring against this parting?

we traveled across the land
towards winter not towards spring

I watched the children become solemn and thin
our wagons and housewares
brittle
            depleted

when I buried my boxes
my watercolors and oils my writing desk

I felt I had given all I could part with:
that was what the desert demanded of me:
then the canyons and boulders

ate at the wheels of our wagons
squeezed the life from our oxen

and we learned to part from our
livestock our friends
our comfort

how can I part with
my sustaining love
who was father

to the whole camp, orphans and families
who whistled us up at dawn

who nooned me in the shade
and fed me at sunset
the darks and lights of his eyes

playing over me like sun and clouds
on a highhearted summer afternoon:

how can I learn to sleep
without his shoulder
to bed down my griefs?

the sun stays hidden
for months the sky has wept its snow

WHERE IS THE WEST

If my boundary stops here
I have daughters to draw new maps on the world
they will draw the lines of my face
they will draw with my gestures my voice
they will speak my words thinking they have invented
           them

they will invent them
they will invent me
I will be planted again and again
I will wake in the eyes of their children's children
they will speak my words

From
Permanent Address:
New Poems 1973–1980
(1980)

A QUESTIONNAIRE

Describe your early education.

> At six, standing on the low stone wall
> beside my grandfather, I was taller than he.
> Wearing my white beret, hair cut short,
> with leather leggings to my knee, I put my hand
> on his shoulder possessively
> and sang him his lullaby, *a moloch veynt,*
> an angel weeps, an angel weeps.

What is your permanent address.

> A flat rock in Central Park
> where an innocent policeman
> found me with my first sweetheart.
> Under Cambridge clocks chiming each quarter hour.
> Beside the sea.
> Beneath Mount Zion.
> On Boston's broad Victorian bosom.
> Across the pond where you are standing, laughing
>   at me.

Male or female.

> Both. When I saw the Greek Hermaphrodite
> I recognized myself and you, each
> two in one. Now I know why
> the Masai warriors grow brave
> by drinking blood and milk.

Are you married.

> Yes, many times.
> I marry my first loves
> over and over. Like coming home.

Describe a crucial event in your life.

> At twenty, I died and was born again. For a while
> I died every day. One day when I was dying
> beside the sea, which ignored me,
> when my guts ran empty and I started sinking
> into that bottomless hollow
> beneath the bed, I suddenly heard
> (through the window, in my head)
> the notes of the *Appassionata*
> calling me back into the world.

List your awards and honors.

> Three children.
> One, a yellow tearose.
> Two, a winedark peony.
> Three, a young fox, heart's desire.

Give a brief statement of your plans.

> To fly.
> To swim across the pond.
> To tell what I know.
> To love you harder.

LIFTOFF

You will make a myth
out of the ordinary
rising beyond your skin
into a new country

        breaking the thin
        filaments of gravity

You cannot elevate
without the hand of wind.
The strong
air stalls in your lungs.

        You hesitate
        on the brink of land.

And in this instant all
the sorrows of obstacle
pause and dissolve.
You lift—

        and, barely moving, skim
        the impossible sky.

WORD

A fur muscle ran across the road.

Only when I saw the pointed tip of it
waving, did I think *chipmunk.*

Sometimes we move inside our bodies
as inside a stranger. The sack
hangs loose, inviting us to think
I can be anyone, go anywhere, do anything.

But once your pen touches paper, all
choices become one, the word as single
as the chipmunk moving in one spasm
from green to *green.*

ARROW

for my son David

The aiming:

you aim at the center of the eye
you gather all landscape around that single point:
    if a bird-ribbon flies across the edge
    if a cloud teases the sun
you gather all to the one point

there is only one

The letting go:

you are let go
you are no longer grasped
empty air surrounds you

you no longer lean against the bow
your hock is free
you are free
you are in danger
remember the center

all of you remembers the center

The flight:

you are moving along an invisible track
(you make it yourself)
straight as your spine is straight
you move forward
air whistles past you
you are speeding towards

(you are gathered
you are pointed
you are free
you are in danger)

the center
of your eye

Yom Kippur: Fasting

The appetite
stirs. On this one day
of the new year
the head becomes light,

without embroideries
of tongue or hand.
Saliva drying, your body
is a transparent cave.

You can see
through the skull into the brain's cavity.
You are a harp for whatever wind
God wants to play.

His music sounds sharper. There is no
barrier between his thought and you.

SOUP COOLS FROM THE EDGES FIRST

Here's the only praise
you can give yourself:
words will obey

you if you listen to them, let
patterns emerge. Otherwise,
nothing will come out as well

as you wish it. Except, when eyes
are not watching, there will rise
deep explosions of joy

from the middle of the earth,
in the dark, mind you,
where the heat still lies.

HOLDING UP THE BRIDGE

The diver under the bay
reports the concrete block
holding up the bridge
is cracked and crumbling.

A narrow road
arches over the water space,
dips towards the shore.
One end of the bridge
goes down on its knees.
Cars and trucks
tumble off like toys.

No.

The diver is lying. Inside
that concrete block
my bones
are holding up the bridge.

> *Three times the builder tried*
> *without the sacrifice,*
> *three times the bridge*
> *shuddered and collapsed.*

> *And then he knew:*
> *only the bones*
> *of his young wife*
> *could placate the girders.*

> *She came, bringing his lunch, singing,*
> *the birds warned her:*
> *that was at Arta,*
> *hundreds of years ago.*

Your bones, my bones, are holding up the bridge.

SEVEN VARIATIONS FOR ROBERT SCHUMANN

1.
I want to explain about the broken finger.
It is all appetite.
Voracious, exuberant, world-
devouring appetite.

When I was five
they found me at dawn beside the piano
playing chords and weeping.
Even when they boxed my ears
for putting a thumb on a black key
it did not diminish my appetite.

I used to place the music
upside-down on the music stand
and laugh at the strange intertwinings
like upside-down palaces
reflected in the canals of Venice.
The notes stare at you
with strange eyes—eyes of
basilisks flowers peacocks maidens.

At twenty, determined to be a virtuoso,
I knew I must risk stretching myself
to the snapping point.

I made a pulley to strengthen
and stretch my hand.

The pulley held one finger up
while the rest played.
I heard the finger snap. I thought
the pain would make me faint. Vertigo.
A crippled pianist.

Who will attempt to reassemble the burst bud?

2.
My mother called music The Breadless Art.

It was my ring finger.

Little Clara, fifteen, eyes enormous
in her delicate face,
played Hummel for me. It was as though
champagne flowed from her fingers. She stroked
my hand, told me not to drink too much beer,
not to turn day into night,
and to write to her.

I write letters of the alphabet
only under compulsion:
I find my real language
in sonatas and symphonies.

She is my hands. My A-major.

I'll fill a balloon with my thoughts
and send it by a kind wind: I'll harness
the butterflies
to dance my two-sided soul to her.

And Clara in answer
will play my new Etudes, saying
she knows no other way
of showing me her inmost heart.
She dares not do it in secret
so she does it in public.

A kiss on the stairway.
A blue dress.

3.
I had a dream of walking beside a deep pool.
I threw my ring into it,
then suddenly longed to fling myself in too.

The need to write is so great,
if I were on a lonely island
in the middle of the sea,
I couldn't stop.

When I published my Opus One,
I felt as proud as the Doge of Venice
when he married the sea—
I now for the first time
married the whole world.

When I wrote my Spring Symphony
my state was like a young mother
who has just been delivered—
light and happy
yet sick and sore.

Clara—now woman, wife, mother, mine—
finds me sometimes very grave.
But I do not allow her to watch me
or practice her piano
when I am composing.

4.
There is a ringing a kettledrumming a trumpeting
inside my head. Heights beckon me,
they want me to jump,
sharp knives terrify me, death is on every side.

Only at night, shored against Clara's sweet body,
now full with our third child,
does the raft stop rocking.

5.
Silence.

      I cannot lift my arm
to conduct. The players before me
seem far away.

I see them
through veils and dim windows.
Their instruments
are crumbling to dust
like old newspapers.

In Venice they asked Clara, after her concert,
"And is your husband, too, musical?"

I hear one note constantly in my head,
one single merciless note,
tuned to A.

They told me a young man had come to call.
Thin, shy, he sat down to play for me.
At once I knew—a genius, a young eagle.
I called Clara to come and hear him.
This is Johannes Brahms, I said,
he is the one
I have been waiting for.

Clara is pregnant with our eighth.

6.

The single note is opening like a flower,
a melody of petals in E-flat major
whispered to me by Mendelssohn, Schubert,
they want me to write it down,
                              no,
                                     the angelic voices
now have the faces of tigers, hyenas
who want me dead, who want me dead—

                    It is raining, it is Carnival,
the ring finger, the ring, I must
throw it into the Rhine, I am sinking beneath
the green mystery, I hear
the secret music.

7.

Locked in this safe place
I sit in the cool garden
making lists
of German towns and cities.

                        It is two years
since I have seen my Clara.

                        It is hard
to move my tongue. Or hands.
But now she is sitting beside me and she
is lovely. I would like
to give her a flower. Or a butterfly.

Brahms is standing behind her.
She is pouring me a glass of wine
and offers it, her hand shaking.
A few drops of wine
spill on her hand.
I lick the drops from her fingers.

Bubba Esther, 1888

She was still upset,
she wanted to tell me,
she kept remembering
his terrible hands:

> how she came, a young girl
> of seventeen, a freckled
> fairskinned Jew from Kovno
> to Hamburg with her uncle
> and stayed in an old house
> and waited while he bought
> the steamship tickets
> so they could sail to America
>
> and how he came into her room
> sat down on the bed, touched
> her waist, took her by the
> breast, said for a kiss
> she could have her ticket,
> her skirts were rumpled, her
> petticoat torn, his teeth were
> broken, his breath full of
> onions, she was ashamed

still ashamed, lying
eighty years later
in the hospital bed,
trying to tell me,
trembling, weeping with anger

MY GREATGREATUNCLE THE ARCHBISHOP

The cossacks snatched him from his mother
at the age of five
to serve in the Tsar's army.

He was farmed with a family
who found him so docile, so bright
they forced him to enter the church.

One day he passed through the shtetl
where he was born, Borisov,
and he heard the sound of a melody,

mournful and familiar.
It haunted him, why was he so shaken by it?
He grew up and became an archbishop.

In the middle of a foursquare
Gregorian chant
he wept to remember

the old Hassidic notes:
di-dona-di, di-dona-di.
They drew him back, back to Borisov,

to the house of his kidnapping.
I am the brother of Yitzie Orkos, he said,
I have heard of my nephew, Yankev Leyb

(that was my grandfather),
he too wants to be enlightened, he has
secretly taught himself Russian,

let me take him, let me educate him:
I have no children of my own.
But they refused,

they denied him,
they were afraid.
It was the time of pogroms.

What was a Russian Orthodox archbishop
doing in their Jewish house?
They sent him away.

Maria Olt

On a hillside in Jerusalem
under the hammer sun, she lifts

a little carob tree, the tree of John
the Baptist, and sets it

into its hole. Solid as a house,
she is called Righteous, a Christian

who hid Jews in Hungary. Her hair clings
around her broad face as she bends

with the hoe, carefully heaping the soil
around the roots. She builds a rim of dirt

on the downhill side and pours water from
the heavy bucket. She waits until the earth

sucks the water up, then pours again
with a slow wrist. The workmen

sent to help her, stand aside, helpless.
She straightens up. Her eyes are wet.

Tears come to her easily.
The small Jewish woman she saved

stands beside her, dryeyed.
Thirtyfive years ago, as they watched

the death train pass, faces and hands
silent between the slats, the girl

had cried, I want to go with them!
No, said Maria, you must understand,

if you go, I will go with you.

THE LANGUAGE OF HILLS

The slope of that hill
is saying something to me,
something diagonal, stony as music.

What is it saying?

Horse.

A bony horse
is grazing on its lip,
white bones on tufted brown.

Does it say *sheep?*

Sheep like stones? No,
but a shepherd moves restlessly
across its haunch.

It says something else:

Weight.
Sky.
It hoists an old city on its spine.

Now I hear:

Trash spills down its shoulder,
bullets, blood,
kicking up the tan dust.

I stumble among the stones,
hearing
footsteps.

Human Geography

The mother rock is black basalt,
hard, handsome.
Walls are made of it, ancient
synagogues, the house of
Saint Peter's mother-in-law.

Climatic conditions:
a rush of new milk,
brief rains, the slow
grinding of wheat,
disappointments.

Bits of rock fall.
Each passing heel
grinds them. They are whipped
by the chamsin, dried
to fecund dust.

From this my children rose.
They were crops, they were trees.
They will squeeze
greengold liquor from olives
ripening by the black wall.

WATCHING THE SUN RISE OVER MOUNT ZION

Orange fish are swimming
over the roofs.

The air is tinseled
with scales of gold.

Someone is coming.

All the harps cymbals violins
drums horns cellos
sing
　　　one blinding note.

The tower is on fire.

It is today.

In the Country of the
Whitethroated Sparrow

1.

two long calls
and three triplets
from a sky of blueberry blue

        now   now
        it is now   it is now   it is now

on an emerald division of earth
we two have come
to a halfmown field

lying circled with pine
we breathe with a sharp first breath
new hay   clover   sun on bark

and the whitethroated sparrow
two-thirds through our harvest
cries   now   now   it is

2.

over the darkening harvest
the sky curves heavy
with silent birds

we come from a room
secure in lamplight
where a trio of Schubert

waterfalls us
into the shaking thunder
long hands of lightning

reach over the pines
thrust above the meadow
and weave us garlands

behind us Schubert sings
over stones glinting through
great sheets of light, it is now

3.

A million kilovolts eat
the dark. We're inside
an electric gale,
watching the white

bones of trees appear
and disappear. The night
is flying metal,
each piece a radiance

of stones, grass, the pillars
of the porch. The neon
sky cracks on and off,
blowing me like wind

against your mouth,
where I am struck to ash.

4.

Time is the mountain that watches over the meadow.
Circling the loved shape in a wedding dance,
we look for a path in thickets of maidenhair,

assault the pinnacle blazed clean by fire,
stretch our lungs in unaccustomed air,
climb across rocks, streambeds, logs,

past trees in second growth, up granite slabs,
muscles in back and thighs reaching
to take the moment, ratify the day.

Breathless above the stunted trees,
above the tangle looking out towards valleys
of promises, somewhere in the pines

below (but seeming high above), we hear
a voice speak prophecy, the sparrow sings
plainly in sheets of light over the peak

not   yet   it will be   it will be   it will be
nudging us gently down, where we must live.
Time is the mountain bending over us.

5.

spaces of sun and shadow
are painted on the grass
again
unlooked for
the season of harvest
in the play of light and morning
your loved shape
moving towards me
through the trees
almost rounding the path
renewed there
coming coming almost
here
the pines dark with longing

6.

a stretto of birdsong:
one cry scissors the air

across the dawn
a crow hones his call

on the granite sky:
two one-notes

echo each other
question and answer

rapid as rain falling:
a cricket adds his bass viol

and the whitethroated sparrow
hidden in pines

waiting for sun
to zigzag through leaves

lets drop half his song
two long calls and a pause

AFTER

The sand was tender,
motherwarm to my feet,

the cleft in the rocks
dazzled my eyes with absence:

the sun pressed down, and the sea
as it rocked in my arms

shamed language
and the language of comfort.

APPLE

Love, on your grave—flat
and strange in the dry grass—
I place a stalk
of red and yellow
everlasting
and prop it
beside your name.

Apple, you called me,
thinking of a girl
round and succulent,
thinking of pink and white
petals blowing their honey
breath over us
that first nuptial summer.

Tomorrow I will bring you
small Rhode Island Greenings,
new red Macintosh
to moisten
your dry sleep.

FOG

       SHE   *HE*

I come to your shore longing

                   you don't notice

for the shape the rise of your land

                   how sunlight sieves

your special rounds and levels

                   through me   you come

but you pull your blanket over your head

                   a large shape

hoping I will think you

                   that parts and breaks

all flat all gray

                   my brooding   you are

a separated mist

                   all troubling

no shore no trees no sky no water

                   waterfall

you pretend that you never

                   all whirlpool

tugged me under your cover

                   you don't see

or drew me down to your contours

                   how I become lost

that you never entered my crevices my

                   in you

long cave and shook me

                   you are final

back to my beginnings

                   I am germinal

you hide from me

                   stop moving

pretending to be blank

                   rest in me

look at me

Rooms of the Ocean

crossing Tiverton bridge to Aquidneck Island

where the Sakonnet river becomes the sea
a flank of water
stretches pewter to the horizon

the morning sun has sucked the sky white
leaving below a blanched gray disk

under the bridge
the river curves northward,
stained a deep irrational blue

I come to the edge where the island begins

a strip of silver foil
a dagger of ocean
glints just beyond Saint George's tower

Second Beach

once on your edge
in your adolescent embrace
I read my summer hunger

I brought my loves to you
one by one
testing them against

your indifference you
my first love and my last
still hiding your secrets

yellow

the sun lowering through the porch windows
rinses everything I look at with little suns
the metallic skin of the ocean
the western air opening wide
reels me into its yellow mouth
as it swallows the rocker, the book
I am reading, the watery golden panes

a veil fell just now

between me and the white ocean

one of the shutters of evening is closing

the blind hands of tides
are feeling their way
below the cliffs and mountains
beneath the forest of water among
the weeds and eyeless fish
along twilight canyons to the

underside of light

the light the face gives off

your aura
when the sun bounces against you
gives me back a sea of flints

even under the shadow
of dwindling boulders
you fling me shimmering nets

without the sun
without the white relief
of your breaking

in night's unclosing eye
I know your face is gathering
is gathering its light again

Singing

1.

three spears of sunlight
lay across the floor

each stream of pointed brass
pierced her throat

2.

she built a tower with her voice

it grew upward
until flocks of chimney swifts
flew in and out of its arches

3.

twelve sandpipers
skittered behind the long lip
of the tide,
pecked at the seaweed:

then skittered back
up the beach
legs trilling
just beyond the wave's bite

4.

sailors rose through her voice
from their drowned boats
drifting up
through the sharp blue of her throat

5.

a chorus of gulls
turned and wheeled
over the full-lunged sea:

the sea sang
basso profundo

it had no doors

6.
they sang together:

she moved
breast first
across the curve of the globe

she arched over
the hidden geography
of the ocean floor

she sailed across
its peaks and resonant valleys

singing

From
The Testing
of Hanna Senesh
(1986)

Hanna Senesh was a young Hungarian poet who immigrated to Palestine in 1939, just as the Second World War began. She helped to found the kibbutz at Sdot Yam, where she planned to work as a farmer, but as news of the Nazi death camps began to spread, she was determined to go back to Hungary to help rescue the remaining Jews and also to help her mother, who had remained in Budapest. In 1944 the British finally allowed her to join a parachute rescue brigade, and she set off on her mission. But it was already too late. The brigade had to land in Yugoslavia because the Germans had already captured Hungary, but Hanna was determined to go on to Budapest. As soon as she crossed the border, she was arrested.

As a little child
I heard a voice

calling me, commanding me:
it was dim at first,

but I knew I was chosen:
it called me, called

until I followed:
now I hear it clearly:

I must be the match
to strike the flame:

I must be the flame

I

Budapest: June 1944

1.

They've been beating me for three days.

My ribs ache.
I think my wrist is broken.
And my jaw is throbbing where the police
knocked out a tooth.

The Gestapo agent was furious
when I threw the book of French poems out of the train
and tried to jump after.
He didn't know the transmitter code was in the book,
he was just angry that I tried to escape.

Now I can't tell anyone the code, even if I wanted to.

2.

After the first shock
it's like letting a wave of flame singe your hand:
first a sharp sensation, then no feeling.
I watch myself like a person in a dream
while they invent devices to break me down.

But I never scream.
Screaming means it's happening to me.
I step back and watch it happen around me.

Anger helps. Anger makes a barrier between the whip
    and me.
They tie me up
and beat my soles, my palms, my back:

                                I say

no   no   to myself
don't let them have a sign that I feel it:

think of the blue-green sea that I saw every night
from my tent under the old stars,
the cool winds of evening:

think of that hill in Jerusalem,
the little lights shining in the villages,
breathe the aromatic Judaean air,
watch the sun set over the Old City,
the shadows creeping up the towers,
pulling the bruised light behind them:

you see: I feel nothing.

It is only my body flopping like a fish.

It is only my body that bleeds.

3.

the self
becomes small and thin
a single taper
burning
        in immense darkness

6.

Trapped in this gray square
I know the earth
is moving across the dawn
from meridian to meridian

all night I keep watching,
searching the walls, the floor
for an opening
into the light:

dreams stream down my face,
my breath stops in my throat,
my bones crush against each other

as I beat at my own absence

II

Yugoslavia: March 1944–June 1944
(*Three months earlier*)

1.

Sitting in the dark inside the plane,
I hear the dispatcher dumping the bales,
each attached to its own parachute.

It's bright moonlight.
we're over Slovenia, which has just been liberated
from the Germans.
                  The partisans
are expecting us. Below I can see
the fires marking the letter E
to show us their position.

It's time to jump.

Every fiber in my body is against it.
But I know that when I let go,
when I let myself fall into open space,
I burst open my limits and feel I can do anything.

The hatch opens.

I jump against the moon.

2.

Stepping out,
I'm delivered to air:
I'm swept into turbulence,
tumbling down
past twenty-five feet
of nowhere:

the laws and patterns of space
unfold my arms and legs:

my parachute blossoms,
a spray of the milkweed,
as my pendulum body
swings beneath it:

now I'm falling slowly,
alive:
I see the trees below me:
I come to the end of sky,
stem first,
ballooning   then collapsing
flower   string   wind:

I cut the cord
and the world is mine

3.

I land on six feet of snow in the moonlight.
It's like falling into a featherbed.

The wind has blown me off course
and I've floated away from the others, out of sight.
As I jumped behind Reuven I heard him curse the pilot
for dropping us on the wrong side of the wind,
away from the flaming E.

I blow the whistle they gave me.
The sound cuts across the silence.
Tall Yugoslav mountains are all around me,
nothing but snow and rock.

Reuven and Abba come out of a patch of trees, shouting,
"There she is!"
We hug each other, laughing with relief.

A band of strange men appear and come towards us,
holding rifles.
Reuven puts his hand on his grenade,
in case we've been betrayed to the Nazis.
But then we see the men are wearing red stars on their
    caps.

They're Tito's partisans.

Standing in the snow, they are barefoot.

4.

The Germans have marched into Budapest.

What will become of the million Jews in Hungary?
They'll be killed by the Nazis while we sit here in the
    snow.

"Reuven," I say, trying not to cry with disappointment,
"What about the plans we made
to help the refugees escape to Palestine?
Let's cross the border now, quickly,
before the Germans bring the storm troopers."

"No," he says, "it's hopeless.
We tried to reach Budapest before the Germans,
but they were too fast for us."

"You mean we were too slow," I say bitterly.
"Why didn't the British arrange to drop us sooner?
The longer we wait, the more impossible it will be.
Let's cross the border now."

"No, Hanna," he says, "it's too late.
You'll only be endangering all of us
and then there'll be no one left
to contact the underground."

"I don't care. It's better to take the risk now
than never to try at all. How can you
sit back and do nothing?"

"That's enough," he says, getting angry.
"You'll get us all wiped out if you keep on like this."

"But we must cross the border. And find a new escape
	route.
Yugoslavia, Hungary, Rumania, are all being shut off.
How can we reach the ships
that will carry the refugees to Palestine
unless we go now?"

30.

I'll cross the border into Hungary
and find my mother
and lead her to safety.

31.

Braided together,
my mother and I
became strong through loss:
she watched my father die
in the bloom of their love,
and her mother, queen of the house,
sicken and slip away.
And then, skillful at parting,
she parted from me.

She let me go, knowing
I would carry her in me
even as she once held me safe
inside her own flesh.

Why then, with her center
in me, this tie
across time and distance,
across death itself,
do I have a longing
so sharp
it digs a hollow
beneath my heart?

35.

There's a fire in me:
it must not go to waste.

Sitting in the snow,
I fan it with my breath.

I cup it in my hands:
it must not be lost.

I am the fire.
I am the moth.

225

III

Budapest: July 1944—November 1944

2.

Mother is in the prison.

Hilda tells me to stand on the chair tower
in front of my window and look across the courtyard.
And there is my mother, waving to me sadly.

I want so much to give her something,
some encouragement, some love.

I look at the dust on the window and slowly, with my
    forefinger,
I draw four Hebrew letters, as big as I can:
shin, lamed, vav, mem—shalom.

She smiles, not understanding.
And then I decide. I will teach her Hebrew.
But how? Something will come to me.

3.

Four letters of the alphabet
sit on my windowsill
like birds in migration:

four sparrows who spiraled
out of the south
on luminous air:

they rest briefly here
before they travel
their half-arc north:

the letters are white
fragments that gather together:
the word is a blessing,

a connecting ribbon
I fling like confetti
across the void

It is to me the Word is speaking

8.

Hilda brings me a few pieces of paper,
a pair of scissors and some colored crayons.
I can't imagine how she got them.

Now I can make paper dolls, little doll pioneers
for the Polish children I see in the courtyard.

9.

Out of thin tissue, hand in hand,
small shapes of boys and girls stand in a row.

I poke my finger through the skin of their world:
it is all made of paper. A puff of breath

could blow it away, could blow away these walls.
Walking up to death, I know I'd find

a hole in the shallow dark, a tear in the veil.
Now my eyes can see the truth of stones:

they are brittle and flat. Transparent. Paper thin.

22.

Not to despair, not to be diminished.

34.

I can see my body shaking, but inside I feel still.

They lead me to a wooden post
under the open sky.
The guard starts to tie me to it.
I say, "No, I'll stand by myself."

He offers me a blindfold.
I push him away.
I'll look at the world as long as I can.

The November air is cold.
If only my body would stop shaking.

I hear a shot, echoing, far away.

Is it meant for me?

I feel myself grow tall tall tall as the sky

35.

I'm standing in the ancient ruins at Caesarea
among the shattered Roman columns
lying in seawater
and I see
the broken statue of a woman
missing entirely above the waist:

but I can tell
from the white hand
lifting the folds of her garment,
from her hard thigh
beneath the fluted skirt,
from the sure grace of her bent knee
and the foot she is leaning on
in its imaginary sandal
the foot
taking her weight

I can tell
she is there

inside the broken body
she is complete.

New Poems:
Laughing Gas
(1980–1990)

EIGHTYTHREE

My mother sits on a towel
on the toilet seat. I dip a cloth
into lukewarm suds and wash her face and neck,
her dry, crevassed neck.

She says, "Sometimes I feel as dark and alone
as before I was born."

I wash her arms, her elbows, the crooks of her elbows,
her underarms.

"That feels good," she says.

I wash her back round and fleshy, the tired
breasts, her belly broad and generous as an old
Renoir. I wash her buttocks, those large apples,
so like my own.

She says, "I'm no good for anybody,
not even for myself."

I wash her thighs and knees, her gnarled toes,
pat her dry, rub her all over with oil.

She says, "Am I your baby?"

Seven Stones
for MHB (1896–1982)

1.

She is not sitting in her chair
not standing at the window
not playing Chopin on the piano
as she did every evening
when I was eleven.

I danced to please her,
awkwardly, but she believed
that I was Pavlova
and that we were both
immortal.

2.

She was afraid of thunderstorms.
When she was a child,
worrying at the window
for her absent mother
who never returned,
weather stabbed all around her.

3.

A garden house
in a deserted resort. New Jersey, 1930.
My mother, young and darkhaired,
reads a story to my little brother and me
about a frog and his transformation
into a man.
            Later I see her crying
among the lattices of the summer house.

4.

The hurricane of 1954.
I lead her to the back of the house
pretending she must wash
my baby's diapers,

afraid she will see
the wind breaking the trees
the murderous ocean
flogging our front windows.

5.
In the shtetl in Russia
everyone knew
death has no reflection.
Her ancestors
covered their mirrors with sheets,
left little stones on the grave,
for remembrance.

6.
I look in my mirror and see her
with bobbed hair and bangs
in a slim long skirt, faintly
smiling, proud and frightened,
holding me, her firstborn, in her arms.

7.
She comes into the room
wearing a blue and white striped blouse,
her dark hair soft around her face.
I think: I must introduce her
to this assortment of shadowy friends
and I hear myself saying, "This is Martha . . . "
as she speaks to me,
some special advice,
some knowledge that will surely untangle
the knot of my life. Her words
are a round breath, a gift of petals,
but I can't catch them, I can't hear her.

THE PROMISE

Last night I found her
waiting alone
in the middle of the lobby
in a strange hotel,
wearing the brown coat
I keep folded in my closet.

She was standing
like a child
lost in a department store,
ready for tears, frightened,
and I threw my arms around her
and held her to me, saying

You will never be lost!
You will always be found!

Waking, I knew my promise
defied the gray ashes
already dissolving in earth,
the late summer cricket
singing, losing its strength,
waiting for me on my doorstep.

Winter is coming. I hoard
the warmth of the sun on my face,
the caress of the ocean
as my aging body
cuts through the water
and comes out shining with salt

and the warmth of motion,
and I swear to her,
as long as I breathe,
whether or not she waits
on my doorstep of sleep,
she will always be found.

The Awakening

An angry horse is facing me,
coming straight at me, eyes wild, the long nose
distorted. On his saddle sits a woman
sprawled backward, her arm lifted in terror
as the stallion gallops out of the frame.

I stared at the scene
in the half-dark of my mother's room,
unable to sleep, sure if I closed my eyes
the crazed horse would burst
out at me through the glass.

A French etching: *Le Lever.*
The horse's head the lifted arm of a servant
standing at the foot of her mistress' bed;
the horse's eye her eye in profile
looking back at her mistress.

She is pulling back the curtain to disclose
a half-clad woman beginning to rise,
her breasts exposed, not knowing her bed
is the back of a horse. By her side
a lover kneels, kissing her hand.

She is reluctant to wake. If I squint my eyes
slightly, I can see the wild horse.

239

FALLING, 1924

Steep marble steps in an old hall.
My brown wicker perambulator
hangs on the top step,
back wheel slipping at the edge,
front wheels dangling in space.

Engine stalled. Motionless. Until

ass over elbow in a whirr of
blankets, knitted booties, pillows,
a smothering hat,—
                    brown wicker
shoots past me.

          A rocket
of birds bursts from the trees,
scatters over the sky
in long spurts of motion
as I fall through the marble air.

ANNA PAVLOVA

for my daughter Rachel

Prepare my swan costume.
—Anna Pavlova's last words.

1.
I'm old,
almost fifty,
but I can still dance the swan.

Without the swan
there is no Pavlova.

2.
On the way to the Marinsky theater
her mother said, "You are about to enter
fairyland."

She was eight years old.

She watched the princess dance the sleeping beauty.
She held her breath.

3.
At twelve
She learned to keep
the middle and little fingers
of each hand extended,
her right hand a mirror copy
of her left.

At sixteen she danced Giselle,
her gauze wings
lifting her from the ground.
The audience stood and cheered,
threw roses, bouquets, wreaths.

4.

My hands are not beautiful,
the fingers a little too thick.

But my ankles are strong,
my arch high,
and I have toes of steel.

When I stand on one toe
the sole of my foot
is an absolute vertical.

The flame spurts up through my feet,
out through the tips of my fingers.

5.

An admirer sent her
a pair of swans.

Jack is her favorite.

His large warm
feathery body
sits in her lap,
his neck curved around
her neck.

Strong Jack,
he could flatten a grown man
with one blow of his wing.

He came to her wild,
flew chest first into a chimney,
and broke it into pieces.

When they found him, twenty miles away
on a strange lake,
they brought him back
and she clipped his savage wings.

6.

I want to be a feather
carried on the least wind,
poised on a breath,
my head proud on my long neck,
my body light, arched,
a whisper of motion.

7.

Arms folded over my breasts,
I float across the stage.
At the brink,
wings outstretched,
I reach towards the horizon,
ready at any moment
to fly.

WRITING IN THE DARK

In her sick bed, in the dark, she laboriously made words on
scraps of paper.
                            —David Porter, *The Modern Idiom*,
                                    speaking of Emily Dickinson

Across the old quilt
my hand gropes
for the stub of pencil.

Blindfolded, I feel my way
over the scraps of islands
I've sewn together:

the old checked tablecloth,
mama's blue dimity,
my gingham pinafore.

I know my life by feel.
Ah, here it is:
my paintbrush, my wand,

my sword. They think
I'm singing the old hymns.
They don't know

how with one stroke
I cut through the fiery bandage
that films my sight

and run through the garden—
my old enemy, the zero,
snapping at my heel.

Fool's Thread

She sews with thread too long for comfort,
out of laziness, impatience, eagerness

to get the task done. Often the thread
swirls and gnarls tight as a spring,

knotting back on itself. Quick at unraveling
tangles, she frees the needle for seam or button

or hem. She refuses to use a thimble.
Her finger keeps the prick mark for days,

but she is proud to confront the chore
without disguise, naked, face to face.

She pulls the optimistic needle through the cloth
while the long tail of the thread

follows snarling behind.

CLARA SCHUMANN

Along the rocky path in the pine woods,
away from the city and her testy father,
she walked behind Robert,
holding the tail of his coat lightly
so as not to disturb him.

Each time he came to a rock
she tugged at his coat,
a playful warning
to keep him from tripping.

I do not want horses or diamonds,
she wrote, but I wish to lead a life
free from care: I am happy
in possessing you, but I shall be
unhappy if I cannot work at my art.
You will need quiet for your composing.
Children will come.
Am I now to bury
my own music?

He strolled, lost in his thoughts,
gazing at birds freckling the sky,
noting the clouds' notations,
while she stumbled across
the rock she had warned him against.

The Meow Woman, Thailand

after a photograph by Walter Kaufman

The brightness in her eyes
comes from a light inside her,
something she is remembering.

An old safety pin
strains her jacket
across her ancient breasts.

Her nose is like my Slavic grandmother's,
flared at the nostrils,
flat and passionate.

Her stubby fingers, like my grandmother's
and like my father's and mine,
are blue and translucent.

She smiles, crinkling up
her wrinkled leather face.
She knows me.

UNCLE HARRY AT THE LA BREA TAR PITS

Against the iron fence surrounding pools
of black asphalt bubbling and boiling up
through geologic layers; against the fence
where this hot tar surprised and swallowed
families of mastodons forty thousand years ago
(their bones now tangled with birds, camels, antelopes,
hundreds of dire wolves and dinosaurs);
where, nine thousand years ago, a young
woman came stumbling across the treeless plain
of Los Angeles, and slipped or was hurled
by a jealous lover into the sticky black lake—
Uncle Harry poses in a jaunty fedora,
his elegant profile turned toward the camera.

> He says, life has cheated me.
> When they shipped me to America
> in 1907, I lost my friends
> and I lost the Russian theaters
> where I stayed every night
> until one or two in the morning,
> adoring the actors.

> A childish prank ruined me.

> I was the smallest of the gang,
> so they hoisted me up
> to hang a black cloth
> over the Tsar's double eagles
> in front of the prison
> while sailors from the Potemkin
> were rioting in the streets.
> Cossacks were clubbing Jews
> left and right. I saw a woman
> running with a baby carriage
> in front of the horses' hooves.

My father said it was Siberia for me,
or America. I boarded a broken-down
ship in Leeds, bound for Boston.

Later I wandered here,
still an exile,
to Elysian Park in Los Angeles.

The feather on his hat is motheaten,
his coat torn and stained,
but he has turned his plucky collar up
like an unemployed actor from Odessa
who knows he is still handsome.
He is ninetythree.

Behind him a lifelike mastodon
made of plaster and acrylic
lifts her tusks in terror
as she struggles half-submerged in tar,
while her mammoth baby
hesitates behind her
on the edge of the black museum.

II

The Drowned Mountain
for CHW (1916–1979)

1. THE MOUNTAIN

A meadow in Vermont, on Bread Loaf Mountain.
I watched you walk with a dancer's quick walk
along the path on the edge of the meadow.
Your shoulders were bent like a scholar's
but your legs were the legs of a dancer.
Your jacket, thick for a hot summer morning,

hiked up on your shoulders. It was the morning
after we spent all night on the mountain
talking in the innocent moonlight, dancing
on the grass. Not wanting me to walk
on the wet ground, you carried me in your scholar's
arms, home at dawn across the meadow.

Smelling of hay and clover from the meadow,
I woke late that August morning
and found you waiting for me, a grave scholar
who knew a mossy cradle on the mountain.
We lay there in the wood. Not a creature walked
by us. Half undressed, learning the dance
of darkness, beside our cooling beer, you danced
hesitantly, as you did in the meadow.
I knew then I would never walk
back without stealing your morning,
without dancing down the mountain
with you, my poet, my curly-headed scholar.

The summer virgin captured the grave scholar,
reluctant or not, and we both danced the dance

of darkness, thigh to thigh on the mountain.
In the full moonlight, back across the meadow,
we found a barn where we could stay till morning.
When the sun was high, triumphantly we walked

back to the ordinary world, where poets walk
and talk in the stilted language of scholars.
But we had learned the dialect of morning;
we had made the star of Venus dance
like a burst of meteors over the meadow,
a wedding beyond time on the mountain.

2. SACHUEST BEACH, 1941

A smell of salt and wild roses all over the island,
red and white roses, the colors of paradise.

We lay, wrapped in one blanket, under the puddingstone
                       rocks
on the west end of the beach. The waves came in
                       slanting

while your mother bent over the fire charcoaling
hot dogs and hamburgers for the others. But we

were oblivious, drunk on salt air, kisses, our own
                       salt sweat.
You were twenty-four, I was nineteen. When everyone
                       left,

the moon rose over the phosphorescent water, a ribbon
                       of gold
that moved with us as we swam. Bubbles of fire

exploded around our shoulders, between our thighs.
We rose together. Mermaid. Merman.

3. The Wedding

In your best friend's car with a borrowed ten dollars
we eloped to Newport, singing over and over
the trial by fire and water from The Magic Flute.
My father cursed us over the phone and threatened
to sit shiva for me as though I were dead.
Your mother howled in the backyard, crying
that you were still a child. My childhood lover
pursued us with a gun. My mother forgave us.

In the morning you sat writing a composition
for your class, describing love and marriage
in Latin, while I went in search of breakfast.
The streets of Cambridge were glistening,
my heart ready to burst like a ripe peach
with love and terror.

4. Basic Training, 1942

I lay stifling on the sheets
    in a rundown rooming house
        in Miami Beach;

you, buttoned up in stiff khaki,
    your curly head shaved
        close as a convict's,

were marching a mile away
    with the typewriter brigade:
        artists, actors, musicians.

You were the only poet.
    You held your gun awkwardly
        while the sergeant

barked and snarled at your heels.
    Sunday we swam among the palms
        in an ocean tepid as a bathtub.

Under a sky askew with unfamiliar stars,
    your friends wept on my shoulder
        for their lost music, their wrenched lives.

Before I left, I ran along
    beside your platoon, shouting
        Look at the sunset, darling!

and every head turned to see
    the sun collapsing
        behind a bloody horizon.

5. COMING HOME DURING THE SECOND WORLD WAR

The train from Denver to Chicago,
from Chicago to Boston. Our 4-F friends
were waiting in the Oyster Bar
at South Station. We drank our way

across the street to the Essex Hotel:
giant martinis for twenty-five cents.
At Hayes-Bickford Cafeteria I threw forks
and spoons in celebration across the counter.

When the subway lumbered over
the old Salt and Pepper bridge
to Cambridge, we greeted the river,
shouting Charlie! Charlie!

I crumpled up on my hatbox near the kiosk
in Harvard Square; you dropped my typewriter,
unable to stand any longer,
laughing and crying.

           We woke
the next morning in someone's livingroom,
sober and jobless, and went out
into the bright Harvard autumn
where headlines reported the rumor
that Hitler was slaughtering the Jews.

6. The Young Scholar, 1952

In the Athens cemetery
the stones lie crumbled
all around us
the sun blisters
the dust, sears
our young heads
as we crouch reading
the old inscriptions

You stand up
among the marble
portraits of mourning
and tense with joy
raise your hand
in the classic gesture
of stone farewell

7. THE SHEPHERD

In Arcadia,
huddled together on a narrow bed,
we conceived a daughter.

I too have dwelt in Arcadia.

I can prove it
by this shepherd's crook
made of olive wood.

Pregnant, I rode donkey back
up the narrow mountain rocks
from Olympia to Bassae,

the temple of Apollo.
An old shepherd
playing his reed pipe

asked us how much money we had
and whether we were millionaires.
You said: We're poor students

traveling on nothing.
He laughed:
All millionaires are liars.

8. SUNION

Sunbathing naked
on the rocks at Sunion
we vowed eternal marriage:

the stern temple,
inscribed with Byron's name,
our only witness.

Doubt
lurked like the octopus
under the rock,

a dark shadow
holding back
under the cliff.

9. THE RUINS OF TIRYNS

High on the peloponnesus of sleep
a stone arch leads nowhere.

Broken stairs.

Where our bodies once touched and turned,
rain gathers in gullies.

Sheep huddle in the gallery,
polishing the wall
with their fleecy sides,
avoiding that same wind
that tore
our mycenaean eyes.

A path slants down to a hidden spring:
to be used only in times of siege.

10. THE DIVORCE

I see your harlot
wearing a black velvet
dress from my closet.

A little play,
you smile, no harm:
a salute to youth, a trifling addition

to your stable of admirers.
You have no permission, I scream,
take that off, it's mine, it's mine,

as you and she turn
and continue walking away.
Why did you come from the grave

into my dream
with your smile, your terrible charm,
unreachable as ever, alive
or dead?

11. THE MINUET

As you lie dying I come into the room
where your second wife and your new mistress
are standing by the bed.

You smile at me like an angel, hold out your hand,
take mine, and cover it with kisses.
Then you stop, look at my new wedding ring,

and bowing your head on my hand, begin to weep.
I draw my hand away, and like a partner
in a minuet, move aside as your mistress

takes my place beside the bed.
The nurse comes in to adjust the plastic bottles.
She looks at the three of us and says:

> *You have many friends.*

> *No*, your wife says, *wives.*

12. THE DROWNED MOUNTAIN

On the lake of our childhood, the lake
shaped like the Caspian Sea,
shadowed by dark Vermont pines,
we drift in a canoe,
you and I and the boy you were.

He slips naked into the water
and you laugh and say, A Greek god!

And then we notice, under the water, under
our keel, a black shape appears
beneath the surface, the shoulder
of a lost continent, a drowned mountain.

Its rocky flanks spread far beyond
where we can see
as we paddle over its secret crevices,
its sunless peak.

The boy swims away and clambers up
on the darkening shore.

I hide from you among the pines.
A silver belt, your wedding gift,
glints around my waist.

You plunge beneath the surface
while the empty canoe drifts away,
your white heel
flashing among the ripples, your white heel
slipping through the sheets.

13. Snow

The sky flat and heavy like old
pewter; the ocean a twin of the sky,
dark gray, like the goblets they sold
to us one day in a Newport junkshop. Why
do I keep talking to you, my
love more sharp to me each year?

The winter's first morning of snow.
The steps of the house, cars hissing on the road
become muffled and still, like your breath.
Slowly the white padding grows
deep, deeper. Has your death
muffled my old rage and fear, the weather
that kept us apart? Together
we drank wine from those goblets, poor
and young.

                 I hardly remember winter here.
Wasn't it always an afternoon in summer,
the sailboats racing on Narragansett Bay,
picnics at Sachuest Point, the saltwater farm
where we heard gunfire practice every day?

Now you are lying under a hill
close beside Bishop Berkeley's chapel
where an eighteenth-century squire and his bride
sleep on their sarcophagus side by side after two
centuries, sculptured in stone, arm in arm
under the snow.

14. THE MATING

I cross the brook
and walk up the hill towards your grave.
A humming fills the air,
a giant motor buzzing among the trees.

Is it the grass growing?
The dead murmuring?

At the crest where you lie
I see in the trees above you, along the edge
of the mausoleum, the air dense with bees
humming loudly, swarming and darting.

The queen is pirouetting with her mate,
performing her act of darkness
under the noon sun.

All our cruelties and denials
all structures of power and frustration
fall like pollen
through the early summer air,
and the simple truth appears:

a wedding, a hint of honey
in the lion's mouth.

III

CRUELTY

This human wind spoils everything
it grazes over, leaving spittle on the floor,

on table tops, pages of books. Rolls
salty hot fog across the bay into

this room. Keeps forcing its damp breath
into my ear, an insistent junta of a wind.

It brings poison from Chernobyl, blight
from our tattered ozone. It insults

the wounded ocean, already scarred with oil,
mimicking its primal essence. It is

without mercy, like the boy carrying
his mother's heart to the sorcerer—

heedless, inexorable—who doesn't hear the heart
cry "Watch out!" as he stumbles through the woods.

MESSENGERS

In my town near the ocean
at nine in the evening
I turn into my driveway
and a baby rabbit
slips from the hedge,
runs across the lawn,
small as a dandelion
in the evening light.

In the morning
by the backdoor spigot
a two-inch toad
hops from a stone
in the salty air:

in this familiar landscape,
anachronistic, doomed,
are they telling me
the newborn will survive,
the young will keep replacing
the persistent dead.

CRACOW

The wizened man in the Jerusalem market cried,
Don't buy a dead fish, buy a live one!
A lebedike: es schvimt, es shpringt, es tantst!
Flapping his arms to show how the live fish
swims, leaps, dances.
We laughed and said, yes, a live one.

He dipped his net into a tub
and brought out a sparkling bewhiskered old man,
flopping and gasping. It sprang to the floor,
unwilling to die.
                    Laughing, he held an ice cube
to the O of its mouth; then holding it down
on his cutting board,
he struck its head with a mallet
and cut it into steaks.

The fish was all bones,
flat and tasteless,
no matter how I cooked it.

Death, too, is a kind of resistance.

Losing a City

The alleys behind the old Jewish market
twist around each other, some paved with
Jerusalem stone, some merely a dirt path for donkeys,
others opening into a sunny white courtyard:
The flash of an orange tree. A box of geraniums.
A gate. A bench. A latticed window.
A few hens scratching in the rubbish.

The phantom pain of a severed limb.

Spiny hills, bitter and inexorable,
sting my feet with absence. Vanished walls,
austere behind the blandishment of roses,
rebuild themselves each night between me
and my exile. I wake, holding my arms
around lineaments that aren't there.

When can I turn the key of my privation
and open a door
into a valley
with olive trees and real brambles.

A GESTURE

The woman clasping her arms around the bearded man's
                                    neck
and leaning on him
is his mother

                his two teenage girls stand apart
                stroking their long hair,
                his teenage boys, each wearing
                a yarmulke and a plaid jacket
                punch each other half-heartedly
                his wife stands aside, embarrassed but docile
                her pretty legs in plain oxfords

but the mother the mother
something about her skirt
her short grayblack hair
her old belted sweater
speaks of Europe, war, deprivation
she is whispering to him
kissing his cheeks he is going away
he is going away
and she has had enough of separation

In the Jerusalem Bakery

The middle-aged woman
in the Jerusalem bakery
gives me warm honey cakes,
braided challahs, small
triangular pockets
filled with cheese and spinach,
crescent-shaped cookies.

She wears a faded dress and over it
a stained white baker's apron.
I see the numbers on her arm.
I try to enter the sadness in her eyes,
in the midst of this sugar,
this cheerful yeast, crumbly pastry.

I greet her, *shalom*, and hand the coins to her
as she stuffs the separate packages
into my net shopping bag. Our hands
touch, our eyes meet, she almost smiles.

In Nazareth

The Arab poet had written, *Little girl,*
do not come near the perilous outposts,
watch out for the barbed fence . . .

Marked as his enemy, I arrived at the hall
where he and I were to read our poems together.
A small whitehaired man
held out both arms as though to embrace me
saying, come, let them take your picture
standing beside me.

In a country where signs in every bus
warn the traveler: BEWARE OF UNMARKED PACKAGES;
where we wait for an hour on Nablus Road
while robot sappers dismantle the bomb;
where police stop every Arab, friendly or not,
demanding to see his papers,
there is every shade of hate, friendship,
shame.

    I'm ashamed of my fear.

Later our picture appears in his magazine,
Arab and Jew side by side,
arms linked across the barbed wire fence
in his poem. The picture is
dim on cheap paper, surrounded by
the words of a veiled language.

FOREIGN TONGUES

We sit around the table
in a Jerusalem suburb,
the bearded Russian painter,
his gentle pear-hipped wife,
and the new cousin from Odessa
with the melancholy eyes.

Each speaks his own language,
Russian Yiddish Hebrew English:

we dip our tongues hesitantly
into each other's words:
yes   lo   kum aher   panamai
we admire the view, complain about
shadowless light on biblical hills.

A double echo of voice and stars
arches over our syllables

and for a moment
we are standing together
at the siege of Leningrad,
the blood from our wounds
turning to red icicles
on the snow.

NET, LAKE, SIEVE

for my students

Here are these mirrors,
one broken, one framed in red,
and three in neat little boxes
that hinge open.

Look at yourselves for one minute.

While you look,
cells are sloughing off,
atoms are multiplying,
the light is changing.

You with your sweet hair
clinging about your face;
you with your loving black eyes;
and you, who have dared
to reveal yourself to me,

look, look hard
into the brittle lake
of our morning.
Only the eye of the mind
can record us whole.

An August Morning

Motionless.
The pines arrested against a wall of sky:
each needle, blade, branch (smelling green
after last night's rain) stops, breath held.

Over this same meadow we have seen
storms flying, lightning, hot winds,
niagaras of birds. But now the season is stilled.

Reversed. As, for the moment, we cease to age.

CHAMBER MUSIC IN EARLY DECEMBER

A cold Sunday morning in early December.
The first snow. All night long the sky
hung heavy with a locked-in gathering flood.
Then at dawn the first snow came.

The first snow. Looking at the sky,
Rachel, who lives twenty blocks away,
sees at dawn the first snow come,
drawing a veil between her house and mine.

Rachel, who lives twenty blocks away
with her cat, her violets, her ballet shoes,
draws a veil between her house and mine.
She unfurls the tender petals of her life

with her cat, her violets, her ballet shoes.
She bakes bread, warming away the snow,
unfurling the tender petals of her life.
Leda returns home from the masquerade,

warm as new-baked bread, despite the snow,
all curves and roses, possible with love.
Leda comes home from the masquerade,
breasts round with soft witchcraft,

curved and rosy, possible with love,
returning as the wheel of seasons turns.
Round with soft witchcraft,
fingers of sun touch our window.

Turning as the wheel of seasons turns,
aging in bed, we come together in hunger.
Fingers of sun touch our window:
we start to perform our feast, our chamber music.

275

Aging in bed, we come together in hunger,
heavy with a locked-in gathering flood.
We start to perform our feast, our chamber music.
A cold Sunday morning in early December.

Your Call

All morning the meagre snow kept falling,
barely whitening the street:

at the window waiting for the soup to boil
I watched a dry leaf pulling on its stalk

and thought how the heart must teach itself to starve—
when your voice—like fire from a star—

burst through the kitchen telephone
and I saw light, sunlight on the branches

as I took you in. Beyond the window
in the empty bushes a sudden bird

wore passionate black and white markings
and a small red crown.

WORD AS WINDOW

I'm looking for the word that will window
your mysterious music, the lovemusic

of Mozart, full of loss, and despite the angry
pain in his belly, hopeful. The music asks

what is so delicate, desirable
as your mouth, your feet, your soft luxurious

shoulder and side, warming my terror at night.
And answers: although flesh will dissolve,

here is the courage to remember; to accept
every stab of memory,—your music

radiating in severe silver streams
through my window, the word merely

the opening. To unlatch.

COLD

Suddenly she wants soft blankets, hot cereal,
tapioca. The damp chill in her spine
ignores the layers of wool she piles on herself
like a poultice.
                Where is the child
who couldn't tell hot from cold; the adolescent
who cavorted naked in front of winter windows;
the nineteen-year-old bride wading in November
in the heedless ocean; the hungry woman
coupling with her lover under autumn hedges?

They are all here, huddled with her under
the comforting quilt, trying to show her how
the heat of the mind can ease the body's ice.

279

OLD LOVE

Familiar, the face you now see
when you look at me belongs to
the young woman perched thirty-five
years ago on the arm of a
sofa, swinging her shapely leg,
wearing a skirt the color of
sunrise. The face is unlined, the
hair long, black, swept into a bun
or braided into a regal
crown. You don't see the cropped gray hair,
the thickened waist or the wrinkled
skin. And I look at you and see
the slender bridegroom pausing at
the door, searching the room, his hair
falling over his eyes, the eyes
bright, hopeful, caressing: you lift
me up and we slide into each
other, young and old, wrinkled, smooth,
like Mozart's Adagio, *con
amore*, tender, heartbreaking.

IN A MIRROR

Sometimes I can see the old woman
in the child, the child in the woman,
a game I play, traveling
in a plane or train, imagining
the businessman next to me a toddler
in diapers, or that mischievous redheaded
infant a woman of forty.

My ages, stacked behind me, blow past
like cards in a hurricane:
the blackeyed four-year-old
with a ball in her dimpled fist;
the fourteen-year-old bathing beauty
with barely defined curves.

But who is this woman in my mirror?
Who is this interloper?
Looking more closely, I recognize
the dark eyes and the high cheekbones,
echoing those ancestors
ravished by the Mongols on the Russian
steppes. In the end it's the bones
that tell who you have been.